# *making* ROOM

# making ROOM

## FINDING SPACE IN UNEXPECTED PLACES

### WENDY A. JORDAN

The Taunton Press

The Taunton Press, Inc., 63 South Main Street, PO Box 5506, Newtown, CT 06470-5506
e-mail: tp@taunton.com

Editor: Carolyn Mandarano
Jacket/Cover/Interior design and Layout: Naomi Mizusaki, Supermarket
Illustrator: Melanie Powell

Library of Congress Cataloging-in-Publication Data

Jordan, Wendy Adler, 1946-
  Making room : finding space in unexpected places / Wendy A. Jordan.
      p. cm.
  ISBN-13: 978-1-56158-802-2
  ISBN-10: 1-56158-802-4
  1.  Storage in the home. 2.  Interior decoration.  I. Title.
  NK2117.S8.J67 2007
  747--dc22
                                  2006017694

Printed in China
10 9 8 7 6 5 4 3 2 1

The following manufacturers/names appearing in *Making Room* are trademarks: Lego®, Star Trek®, Thermafiber®

## DEDICATION

*In loving memory of my father, Arthur M. Adler, Jr., the world's best!*

## ACKNOWLEDGMENTS

The projects in Making Room are the work of a wide range of talented people—from architects, designers, and residential remodelers to homeowners with a creative eye and a skilled hand. My thanks to them all for sharing their ideas with me and allowing me, in turn, to share those inspirational ideas with the readers of this book.

Members of numerous trade organizations, including the American Institute of Architects, the American Society of Interior Designers, the National Kitchen & Bath Association, and the National Association of the Remodeling Industry, came forward with wonderfully innovative projects that enrich these pages. Additional industry professionals provided help in the form of information. I am grateful for all of their contributions.

Thanks go as well to the editorial professionals at The Taunton Press who worked with me. Editor Carolyn Mandarano, along with Wendi Mijal, Julie Hamilton, Jennifer Peters, and others helped ensure that this book met the high standards of practical content and polished design for which Taunton is noted.

And I'd like to thank my family and friends for their support and interest while this book was coming together. I've been excited about the book all along; thanks for sharing that excitement.

# contents

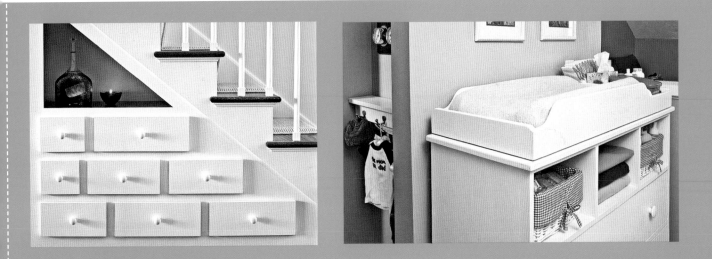

# INTRODUCTION

We ask a lot of our homes. We used to be content with houses that were bundles of boxy, single-purpose rooms, sprinkled here and there with a few closets. That won't cut it anymore. Today we want versatile living spaces that have a place for all our activities, all our high-tech equipment, and all our varied belongings.

Much has been written about the major remodeling projects and spectacular additions that all of us admire. But it's no surprise that, after reading about these impressive makeovers, many homeowners become discouraged. They assume that to get what they need they have to build an expensive addition or perhaps move to a larger home.

*Making Room* shows that there is another option, one that is easier, faster, and much less expensive. That option is to make the most of every inch of unused or underused space you already have. Of course, in most homes, surplus space is limited. Nevertheless, smart use of even the slimmest of spaces can make a dramatic difference in the function and livability of a home.

I made two discoveries as I researched this book. First, just about every homeowner is hungry for ideas on how to "make room." Whether they live in old or new houses, small condos or three-story Victorians, and whether they've lived there for years or just moved in, people are eager for tips on finding and using all the available space in their homes.

Second, there is a wealth of truly wonderful ideas for use of such spaces. Architects, designers, and remodelers may not keep files on reclaimed-space projects as they do for kitchens, baths, and other more established remodeling categories. But, boy, do they have such

projects—all kinds. Homeowners can be marvelously inventive, too. Many of the ideas on these pages came from individuals who devised clever ways to capture slivers of space in their own homes.

As you go through this book, I encourage you to consider what it tells you about your house. With *Making Room*, you can learn where to look and how to identify good spots for built-ins and space-conserving structures that add value and interest to a room. You will discover innovative ideas for transforming niches, closets, and hitherto hidden spaces into functional, personality-filled places. And you will pick up practical information to use in implementing these ideas.

*Making Room* is about challenge and about opportunity. It challenges you to look—really look—at the spaces around your house. I guarantee that the search will uncover pockets of space that have not yet been put to work. That in turn presents an exciting opportunity—the chance to make your house more efficient, more convenient, more distinctive, and more enjoyable.

# *found*SPACE

Want more space in your house? Chances are you already have it. I'm talking about overlooked, underperforming, or hidden space—"found space" that can be put to productive use in creative ways. Less time-consuming and certainly less expensive than adding on, transforming existing space you didn't even know you had has twin benefits: It fulfills a need and makes you feel like you got the bargain of the year. If you think you've maximized all the space your home has to offer, read on. Untapped spaces can be discovered in almost every room, giving you the flexibility to add new features wherever you need them.

## WHO DOESN'T WANT MORE SPACE?

Why focus on found space? The better question is "Why not?" By its very nature, found space adds function without taking up space that's already in use in the house or requiring you to give up part of your yard for an addition. And capturing hidden or overlooked spaces enables you to add elements to a room without stealing an inch of floor space. An added bonus comes from adapting underperforming rooms for fresh, productive uses. When you do this, you "clean house," eliminating wasteful space and improving the overall efficiency of the house.

Using found space is smart for financial reasons as well, especially compared with the expense of a typical addition. On top of the emotional cost of having your house—and your life—torn apart, additions entail a suite of pricey elements that found space projects don't, like the removal of exterior walls and the addition of new footings, exterior walls, windows, and roofing. Also, found space projects tend to be quick—they require a week or two at most—translating into a savings in labor costs. Besides, many found-space projects are simple enough for homeowners with basic carpentry skills to undertake on their own. What's more, most of these enhancements to the home don't result in higher property taxes; they simply add livability to the property.

### Art Work and TV in One

There's no need for the plasma TV to displace artwork over the fireplace. Commercially available systems make it possible to cover the TV screen with art or project a display of photos on the screen itself.

With an art-screen system like the one shown here, a picture frame surrounds both the fabric art screen and the TV screen hidden behind it. When you want to watch a movie, just push the button on a remote, and the art screen retracts onto a roller to reveal the TV. You can choose pictures for the art screen from the manufacturer's catalog or have one custom-made from your favorite poster or large photo.

To meet code, the installation shown here includes a projection above the tile that contains a layer of cement board to separate the firebox from the TV.

## DISCOVERING SPACE

Think of the discovery process as a creative challenge. Take a tour around your house, looking for areas with expansion potential. Some untapped spaces in a house are whole rooms waiting to be transformed. Others are small pockets—a few feet or even a few inches. But don't disregard these tiny places. They can represent remarkable opportunities for innovative storage solutions and other enhancements of the living space.

You may have rooms that are not being used efficiently—a family room, for instance, with "dead" corners and an amorphous core. Organizing a room like this into cleverly delineated zones for entertaining friends or sitting around the TV will make the space instantly feel more dynamic. Smaller rooms have exciting potential, too. Efficient built-ins can pack a surprising amount of function and character into a room, regardless of its size. Do you have a nook or low-ceilinged under-eave area somewhere in your house? If so, you're in luck. A cozy place like this can be the ideal spot for a computer center, a play space, or a bed alcove. And check out your closets. Perhaps one or two can be repurposed to become a home office, craft center, or snack bar.

❶ **A LOW PLATFORM** and a wraparound shelf are enough to delineate the "bedroom" in this attic apartment. The bedroom space is too small to be enclosed behind walls; this subtler treatment defines a private corner without sacrificing the openness of the room.

❷ **THIS SMALL CABIN SPACE** is essentially one room, but it functions as three. Standard-height walls shape a little bedroom with a space-saving pocket door in a corner of the living space; a second bed fills the "garret" above the bedroom ceiling. The skylight adds to the coziness of the garret space while beaming sunlight into the living area.

## Create Your Own Toolkit

With these basic tools, you will be equipped to handle most small construction projects such as the ones in this book.

### Planning and Design

- ◉ Graph paper
- ◉ Level—a carpenter's level or a smaller torpedo level
- ◉ Square—a carpenter's square or a more versatile combination square
- ◉ Stud finder
- ◉ Tape measure—25 ft.

### Construction

- ◉ Circular saw or cordless utility saw
- ◉ Claw hammer
- ◉ Crowbar
- ◉ Handsaws—two or three of different sizes
- ◉ Pliers—several, including slip-lock, needle-nose, and vice-grip models
- ◉ Power drill—with screwdriver bit and perhaps other accessories, such as a sanding disk
- ◉ Screwdrivers—a set of standard and Phillips-head types in a range of sizes
- ◉ Safety goggles
- ◉ Steel ruler
- ◉ Utility knife
- ◉ Wire cutter
- ◉ Wrenches—a set that includes a range of sizes

**❶❷ BUILT-IN CABINETS** form a bed alcove and incorporate a room's worth of storage. The super-organized cabinetry houses a combination of shelves, drawers, and hanging rods carefully planned to accommodate the homeowner's belongings; side niches work as night tables.

**❸ HERE'S PROOF** that everything a child needs can be packed attractively into a small bedroom. This 8-ft.-long built-in in a boy's bedroom includes a bed platform atop storage drawers and rollout guest bed, a tall cabinet with bookshelves in front and toy cupboard/headboard behind, and a bureau and display shelves at the foot of the bed. There's even a reading light.

**❹❺ THE TOP TIER** of the bed platform contains deep drawers for clothes and toys; a look-alike beadboard panel across the bottom tier flips up to reveal a trundle bed. Behind the bookcase is a toy cabinet accessible from the child's bed.

Some of the most promising untapped spaces are hidden from view. In most kitchens, for instance, there is a gap between appliances and the adjacent base cabinets. You can use this space for a slim pull-out cabinet to store your spices. There's expansion potential behind walls, too. Wall cavities between studs may be just 6 in. deep, but that's enough for shelves. And the space between studs often is considerably deeper, opening opportunities for recessed cabinets and bookcases. A staircase with no well behind it for another stairway is a spatial bonanza. You may find room under your stairs for a media center, desk, or playhouse. Even the stairs themselves can be transformed, making way for secret drawers.

## Stock Product, Custom Use

**With ingenuity, ready-made products can be adapted for inventive new uses. In this kitchen, a standard cabinet front is a key component of a cleverly designed trash compartment that occupies an awkward, hard-to-use under-counter area and blends with the rest of the cabinets in the room.**

The homeowner contacted the cabinet company to order a standard angled base cabinet front as well as a matching filler panel. He spliced the two pieces together to make a front that matched the odd shape of the under-counter area. The assembly is attached to the adjacent cabinetry with a piano hinge.

The front came with a door and a drawer front. The homeowner adapted the drawer front, hinging it to the cabinet front to make a pull-down door. Then he made a sheet-metal chute whose opening lines up with the little door. Recyclable bottles and cans can be tossed through the "drawer" opening and down the chute. Other trash is dropped into a plastic bin just inside the regular cabinet door. When it's time to take out the trash, the whole cabinet front swings open so the bin and chute can be removed.

1. 6-IN.-WIDE FILLER PIECE
2. PIANO HINGE
3. 19-IN. X 5$\frac{1}{2}$-IN. DRAWER FRONT ON TWO STANDARD "WAINSCOT CABINET" HINGES
4. 19-IN. X 24-IN. CABINET DOOR
5. STANDARD 36-IN. BASE CABINET FRONT
6. SHEET METAL CONTAINER FOR BOTTLES AND CANS
7. PLASTIC TRASH CAN
8. 18-IN.-DEEP SIDE PANEL (THE OTHER SIDE OF THE TRAPEZOIDAL OPENING IS 24 IN. DEEP)

## PLANNING THE PROJECT

Once you've identified extra space in your home, you're ready for the next step—assessing its potential. You'll want to measure the space to determine if it is suitable for the use you envision. "Standard Sizes" on p. 16 lists the typical dimensions of components for many found-space projects. Check your local building codes for additional spatial requirements, such as ceiling height and door clearance. If you plan to build into a fireplace wall or extend plumbing lines, you will need to get information about codes pertaining to distances and clearances in these areas, too.

❶ THE CORNER SPACE in a string of cabinets is deep—so much so that it can house a multibin recycling center in this kitchen. One 44-qt. and two 28-qt. receptacles line up in a clear-coated birch drawer that's attached to heavy-duty drawer glides; side braces stabilize the big bin and support the drawer front.

❷ A HIDDEN SPICE RACK fits into the 8-in. gap between the cabinet and the corner under this kitchen counter, tapping space that's usually left empty. Full-extension drawer glides bring the three shelves into full view; when the rack is closed, it looks like a stationary panel. All the ash cabinetry in this kitchen is custom, but similar spice rack inserts are available as standard options.

❸ THE COLUMNS flanking this range are both elegant and efficient: Behind them are full-extension pullouts that provide bonus storage. One of the 5½-in.-wide pullouts contains shelves for spices and cooking oils; the other houses hooks for a towel and the kitchen scissors, plus twin magnetic strips to keep knives handy and securely in place.

**1** THE WALL BETWEEN vanity and tub in this bathroom bridges the corner gracefully and also creates a convenient storage place. A tall, deep niche built between wall studs keeps towels within reach of both the tub and the sinks.

**2** HANGING ON HOOKS in a recessed wall cabinet, large skillets stay organized and easy to find. The 16-in.-deep cabinet also features adjustable shelves. Even with all that storage, the cabinet absorbs no floor space and is hardly noticeable when the flush door is closed. The top of the cabinet interior is $3/4$-in. plywood to support the heavy-duty hooks.

## Standard Sizes

Keep these typical dimensions in mind as you measure the available space in your house and make plans to put it to use. Custom sizes are always an option.

### In the Bathroom

● Bathtubs—tubs vary in size and style, but they typically are 32 in. wide and 5 ft. long.

● Countertops—vanity tops usually are 18 in. to 21 in. deep; the standard height is 32 in., though many people prefer 36-in.-high counters.

● Doors—bathroom doors generally are 2 ft. 4 in. wide.

### In the Kitchen

● Appliances—most under-counter units are no more than 26 in. deep and fit beneath a counter that is 36 in. high.

● Cabinets—base cabinets typically are 36 in. high and 24 in. deep; wall cabinets typically are 12 in. to 15 in. deep; most stock cabinets come 18 in., 24 in., or 36 in. wide.

● Countertops—the standard kitchen counter is 36 in. high and about 1 in. deeper than the base cabinets.

● Workspace—wall cabinets are placed at least 15 in. above the counter to allow room to use the counter and 24 in. above the cooktop.

### Around the House

● Beds—standard mattress sizes vary a little but generally are as follows: crib—28 in. by 52 in.; twin—39 in. by 75 in.; double—54 in. by 75 in.; queen—60 in. by 80 in.; California king—72 in. by 84 in.; eastern king—76 in. by 80 in.

● Bookcases—shelves are usually 10 in. to 12 in. deep and spaced 8 in. to 15 in. apart; shelves for CDs can be 7 in. deep and as little as 6 in. apart. Shelves made of $3/4$-in. wood can be up to about $2^1/2$ ft. wide without requiring additional support.

● Desks—the typical desk height for adults is 28 in. to 30 in.; desks for small children are 20 in. to 25 in. high (or full height, with an adjustable chair and footrest); the keyboard surface should be at a height that the user can reach comfortably with elbows at a right angle.

● Doors—a range of standard door sizes is available, but these sizes are common: closet—2 ft. to 2 ft. 4 in. wide; passage—2 ft. 6 in. to 2 ft. 8 in. wide. For pocket doors, keep in mind that a wall cavity deep enough to house the doors and hardware assembly is required. (Pocket door assembly kits are commercially available.)

● Dressers—low dressers generally are at least 26 in. high; bureaus are 29 in. to 50 in. high.

**❸** STAIRS CAN DO double duty as storage compartments. Convert the treads to flip-up lids or insert drawers underneath. With no stairwell behind this staircase, there was room in the lower steps for 3-ft.-long drawers; extra-long drawer glides make every inch of storage space accessible.

A stud finder will help you locate the wall studs so that you know where the supports and between-stud spaces are. If you plan to open, modify, or remove a wall, you'll first need answers to several questions about the wall: Is the wall load-bearing? Can studs be cut to enlarge the space? How will the load be adequately supported once the space has been opened? It is wise to consult an engineer or construction professional to help figure out what can and can't be done before you pick up a hammer or crowbar. Indeed, when wall modification or plumbing and electrical systems are involved, you may choose to delegate your project to a builder or remodeler; the extra cost will be balanced by peace of mind.

What materials will you need and how much will they cost? You have wide latitude here. You can use all-new materials, incorporate salvaged or scrap parts—an especially good option for small projects—or include ready-made or ready-to-assemble components. You can stick to standard sizes or opt for custom-size elements that may cost more but work better in the space. "Wood Primer" on p. 18 identifies the types of lumber and wood products you may need. "Resources on the Web" on p. 13 can help you select the products for your project, assemble a list of materials, and develop a rough estimate of materials costs.

Throughout the book, you'll find information on readily available products specifically designed for small spaces. Another innovative option is to order ready-made parts and customize them yourself. The results can be quite wonderful; see "Stock Product, Custom Use" on p. 14.

## FINDING INSPIRATION

As for finding inspirational ideas for use of the space in your house, you've come to the right place. This book is a treasure trove, a compendium of eye-opening projects that capture and celebrate found space. Dozens of projects are presented with detailed descriptions, sketches, construction tips, and suggested adaptations to make the ideas fit your needs and dreams. Scores of additional ideas are showcased in idea galleries.

Creative use of found space adds far more than inches to a home; it brings new usefulness, style, and delight. Make the most of the space you have by bringing the ideas presented in *Making Room* to life in your home.

**❶ THE SPACE** under these stairs is a multifunctional storage mecca, but the wall still looks sparse and clean. Cabinet doors melt into the bead board (the lowest door even continues the baseboard), so the white wood expanse is punctuated only by the art niche and bookcase. But behind doors are two 3-ft.-deep cabinets—a toy garage and a TV-stereo center—plus a coat closet to the right of the bookcase.

**❷ ENCLOSING THE STAIRWAY** visually extended the warm, wood-paneled wall in this old house, making the space feel bigger and less irregular. Almost hidden in the expanse of painted paneling is a large under-stair cabinet featuring a cupboard and six drawers.

**❸ FIT FOR A KING,** this boy's bedroom finds space for a king-size bed by perching it on stilts. The generous dimensions of the bed platform scribe a spacious study underneath, too. Integral to the cabinetry, the bed loft is bolted to the wall for firm support; built-in bed rails should be added for safety.

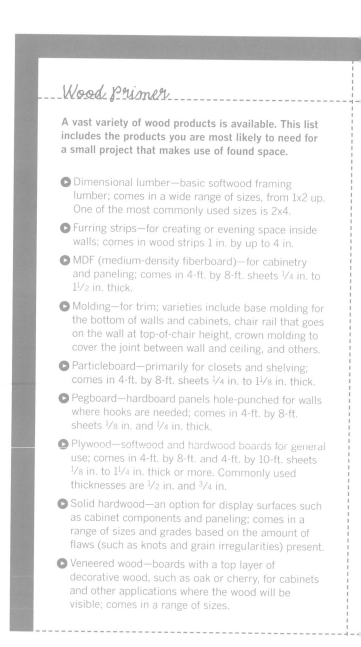

## Wood Primer

**A vast variety of wood products is available. This list includes the products you are most likely to need for a small project that makes use of found space.**

- ▶ Dimensional lumber—basic softwood framing lumber; comes in a wide range of sizes, from 1x2 up. One of the most commonly used sizes is 2x4.
- ▶ Furring strips—for creating or evening space inside walls; comes in wood strips 1 in. by up to 4 in.
- ▶ MDF (medium-density fiberboard)—for cabinetry and paneling; comes in 4-ft. by 8-ft. sheets 1/4 in. to 1 1/2 in. thick.
- ▶ Molding—for trim; varieties include base molding for the bottom of walls and cabinets, chair rail that goes on the wall at top-of-chair height, crown molding to cover the joint between wall and ceiling, and others.
- ▶ Particleboard—primarily for closets and shelving; comes in 4-ft. by 8-ft. sheets 1/4 in. to 1 1/8 in. thick.
- ▶ Pegboard—hardboard panels hole-punched for walls where hooks are needed; comes in 4-ft. by 8-ft. sheets 1/8 in. and 1/4 in. thick.
- ▶ Plywood—softwood and hardwood boards for general use; comes in 4-ft. by 8-ft. and 4-ft. by 10-ft. sheets 1/8 in. to 1 1/4 in. thick or more. Commonly used thicknesses are 1/2 in. and 3/4 in.
- ▶ Solid hardwood—an option for display surfaces such as cabinet components and paneling; comes in a range of sizes and grades based on the amount of flaws (such as knots and grain irregularities) present.
- ▶ Veneered wood—boards with a top layer of decorative wood, such as oak or cherry, for cabinets and other applications where the wood will be visible; comes in a range of sizes.

# SPACE *behind* WALLS

Knock into walls—don't tear them down—to capture unused space that can make any room live larger.

# KITCHEN *bump-out* INTO THE GARAGE

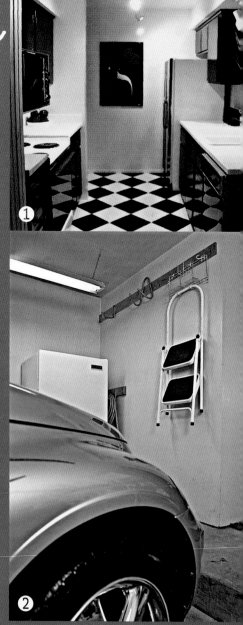

*Who doesn't need more space in the kitchen? This homeowner found a ready solution—reassigning a portion of the adjacent garage to be part of the kitchen.*

The kitchen extension was constructed like a big closet, sized specifically to enclose the refrigerator (moved from a different location in the kitchen) and an adjacent pantry. The pantry is big enough to house two walls of shelves and a side wall full of bins and racks. Everything from cookbooks to small appliances to foil and fire extinguisher has an assigned place. Rather than waste the sliver of space above the refrigerator, it was put to use as a garage for platters and trays.

Moving the refrigerator opened the way for an extra run of countertop plus new base and wall cabinets. And the refrigerator's new location facing into the kitchen improves the stove-sink-refrigerator work triangle.

As for the garage, the new wall offered ideal storage space for ladders, brooms, and rakes, and there's still room for an upright freezer.

**❶ BEFORE** The original corridor kitchen squeezed a mishmash of counters and cabinets onto two walls, and the refrigerator bulged into the room.

**❷ THE NEW GARAGE WALL** contains hooks and carriers.

## MAKE IT *yours*

Create a work center/recessed desk instead of a pantry next to the refrigerator. Order small shelves and cabinets to match the trim, and box around the refrigerator to give the space a total built-in look.

Carve out a laundry area by borrowing garage space. House the washer and dryer in cabinets that blend in with the rest of the kitchen or install bifold doors around them.

Create a recycling center by adding a small door or sliding panel in the back wall of the pantry that is accessible from the garage. Keep trash bins in the pantry area so they can be brought in and out easily.

**❸** AFTER Two-tone cherry doors and rails match the new kitchen cabinets.

**❹** SHELVES AND RACKS fill two walls of the pantry, and a faux-painted shelf of spatter ware disguises a bulkhead at the top.

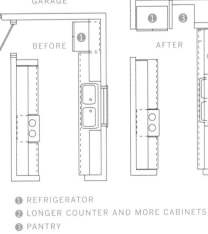

GARAGE

BEFORE

AFTER

❶ REFRIGERATOR
❷ LONGER COUNTER AND MORE CABINETS
❸ PANTRY

FLOOR PLAN

# *built-ins* SHARED BY TWO ROOMS

When the homeowner decided to convert a small first-floor bedroom to an office she wanted to add storage without giving up floor space. In the adjacent bathroom, a bulky vanity hogged space. Built-ins that share wall space between the two rooms solve both problems.

Part of the office cabinetry is the full 31-in. depth of what was a bed niche—deep enough for rolls of blueprints, a small television, and other large items. But the bookshelves and cabinets for general office supplies are only half as deep as the niche, leaving room to open the wall and build the bathroom vanity behind them in the remaining inches.

The new vanity is lean, with a top that extends just a few inches beyond the niche, freeing up floor space in the bathroom. And it's long, making room for four cabinets and two drawers. A partition built between tub and toilet adds more storage in shallow shelves and provides privacy without blocking light from the window.

**❶ MORE THAN 5 FT. WIDE,** the vanity features a countertop with ample space on both sides of the sink. Filling the back wall with a mirror makes the room feel even bigger.

### FLOOR PLAN

❶ BATH VANITY
88 IN. HIGH,
64 IN. WIDE TOTAL
(55-IN.-WIDE OPENING),
15 IN. DEEP

❷ PARTITION
61 IN. HIGH, 38 IN. WIDE,
5 IN. DEEP
(SHELVES 4¼ IN. DEEP)

❸ VANITY TOP
34½ IN. HIGH,
21 IN. DEEP (INCLUDING 6-IN.
EXTENSION BEYOND NICHE)

❹ VANITY CABINETS
18 IN. DEEP

❺ OFFICE

❻ OFFICE BUILT-INS
88 IN. HIGH, 104 IN. WIDE

❼ SHALLOW CABINETS
15 IN. DEEP, 22 IN. WIDE

❽ SHALLOW BOOKSHELVES
AND DRAWERS
15 IN. DEEP, 44 IN. WIDE

❾ DEEP CABINETS
31 IN. DEEP, 22 IN. WIDE

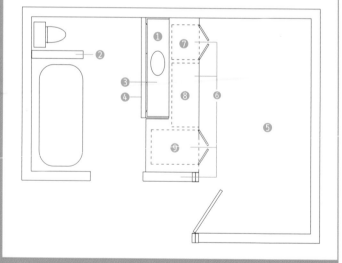

The office built-ins look neat when the cabinets are closed, but they're hardworking and well equipped on the inside. Adjustable shelves in the upper cabinet on the deep side store plans and assorted product samples. The television sits on a pullout shelf in the deep cabinet below; outlets and cables for the television and VCR occupy the cabinet, too. The shallow cabinets and drawers contain typical office supplies—paper, pens, scissors—plus outlets for the phone charger and electric pencil sharpener.

All told, the office ensemble boasts eight drawers, four cabinets, and a large bookcase. That's plenty for this home office, and it's equally appropriate for a bedroom, in case the room changes jobs again.

Install a shelf extension that operates like a keyboard drawer for auxiliary workspace.

Add a closet with shelves instead of deep cabinets.

Insert shallow shelves or cabinets in the side panels above the vanity.

Put shelves on the tub side of the partition for a soap dish, shampoo, and washcloths.

Install a recycling and trash unit between a kitchen and bathroom, leaving 4 in. in the bathroom vanity but allowing the kitchen to gain efficiency.

❸ THIS OFFICE WALL ENSEMBLE features cabinets and drawers that wrap around a central bookcase. The flush-front cabinetry hides the variation in depth.

❹ THE BEAD-BOARD BACKING helps the bookcase in the shallower portion of the ensemble to blend with the style of the house, a 1920s bungalow.

# *recessed* ATTIC FURNITURE

Turning an attic into a livable room often means writing off space under the eaves because walls are erected several feet inward, where the sloped ceiling allows adequate height for standing.

This kids' room demonstrates a better strategy. With the goal of recessing a bookshelf 3 ft. above the floor to act as a ledge behind each bed, and ensuring that the wall would be at least 5 ft. tall to meet code, the designer sketched out right triangles from the eave. When the needed height and clearance was formed by the triangles, he knew where to place the new wall.

The maple bookshelf is 10 ft. wide, making it long enough to run behind two twin beds. Though it really is just one long box recessed in the wall, it has a central divider that gives each child a shelf of his own.

Each child also has his own recessed bureau: The triangle that allowed room for the bookshelf also made space for these four-drawer bedside cabinets. Stained and trimmed to match the bookshelf, the bureaus help organize the bedroom and put things away—even the furniture.

**❶ THE 5-FT. WALL** built a few feet in from the eaves houses a wide shelf and two four-drawer bureaus.

**❷ THE BUILT-IN BUREAUS,** which are 4 ft. high and 2 ft. deep, hold a lot and take up no floor space.

❶ ANGLE AT CEILING APPROXIMATELY 10/12 (10 IN. HIGHER FOR EVERY 12 IN. IN LENGTH)

❷ 5-FT.-HIGH INTERIOR WALL

❸ 24-IN.-DEEP DRAWERS IN CABINET, 48 IN. HIGH

ATTIC

Install a painted or stained bureau in the wall opening. Finish the frame in a complementary or contrasting stain or paint.

Design a wall insert with open shelves, drawers, cupboard space, and perhaps a pullout desktop.

Integrate reading lights into the book ledge.

Include outlets for a radio, clock, and cell-phone charger.

# LAUNDRY ROOM *niche*

*The typical side-by-side washer and dryer dominate whatever room they're in, bulging out from the wall. Not here. The machines in this sunroom/breakfast room recede through the wall into a bathroom, effectively shrinking to half their depth.*

The twin machines extend only 12 in. into the sunroom; the rest of their 28-in. depth is behind the wall. In the sunroom, the machines are topped by a 36-in.-high solid-surface counter. A ready-made 24-in. cabinet end piece was split in half to make the end panel for the appliance cabinet, and a coordinating in-cabinet divider was inserted to separate the washer from the dryer.

In the bathroom, the backs of the machines protrude through the wall about 8 in. A 14-in.-deep strip of cultured marble acts as a countertop, creating a useful extension of the vanity top. The machines hide behind cabinet doors that match the others in the bathroom. The cabinet creates a storage place for toilet paper and extra cleaning supplies, and it provides machinery access that will delight the appliance repairman.

① 

❶ **RECESSING THE WASHER AND DRYER** into the wall saves a lot of floor space. The 14-in.-deep counter above the front-loaded machines is big enough for practical use.

❷ **ON THE BATHROOM** side of the wall, the machines hide behind doors that match the other cabinetry.

❸ **ACCESS TO** the machinery and hookups, often a problem with washers and dryers, is easy here.

## MAKE IT *yours*

Recess a stacked washer-dryer unit into the wall, backing it up with a broom closet or pantry.

Stack a washer-dryer unit adjacent to the refrigerator by facing them into opposite rooms. Put shallow cabinets or shelves behind each appliance.

Add a gas fireplace insert to an interior wall and back it up with a shallow cabinet or just a cabinet door face. (Check local codes regarding fireplace insulation and clearances.)

# DRESSER AND SIDEBOARD *in one*

Space was tight in their small bedroom, but the homeowners really needed a bureau. They also wanted a sideboard in the dining room, but there wasn't room for a big one with cabinets inside. Inserting cabinetry into the wall between the rooms gave them a dining room sideboard and a bedroom bureau all in one.

In the bedroom, the bureau is flush with the wall and is wide but low, to fit beneath the buffet counter on the dining room side of the wall. The slim buffet is just 12 in. deep, but adding the thickness of the wall gave the bureau drawers a respectable 18 in. from front to back. Full-extension drawer slides make every inch of those drawers accessible.

The sideboard blends gracefully with the other furnishings in the dining area. It's the same height as the countertops that cover the cabinets along another wall, and it's constructed of the same distinctive red birch. Dark granite tiles make a handsome, heat-resistant buffet surface.

A few tricks make inches go far on the sideboard. The countertop extends an inch or so beyond the cabinet on the front and sides. And the short granite backsplash gives the illusion of added depth.

❶ **THE BEDROOM DRESSER** takes up no floor space; its 18-in.-deep drawers are encased completely inside the dining room sideboard.

❷ **ADDING AN INCH** around the edges of the countertop gives the sideboard a generous 13-in.-deep buffet surface.

## MAKE IT *yours*

Insert a bookcase instead of drawers into the wall space in the bedroom.

Install shallower cabinets or shelves back to back on both sides of the wall.

Fill the opening with side-by-side cabinets, one facing the dining room and the other facing the room on the other side of the wall.

# SLIDING CLOSET
## *in a wall*

*A shortage of closet space is something most homeowners have to deal with. The owner of this house discovered room for a hideaway closet that surfaces only when needed.*

No space could be spared for a closet in this second-floor room. The homeowner uses it primarily as an art studio, so the walls are filled with paintings. Several feet along one wall were reserved for a bed for houseguests. Of course, the guests would need a closet, but building one into this compact 12-ft. by 9-ft. room wasn't an option.

Above the guest room is a small loft, and on the other side of the guest room wall is the cathedral ceiling of the first-floor living room. After some exploring, a 3-ft.-deep cavity was found sandwiched between the floor of the loft and the ceiling rafters of the living room. While the cavity could not house a conventional closet because it cleared the rafters 14 in. above the guest room floor, it could house a closet-size cabinet.

Basically an upright drawer, the closet slides into the wall cavity. When closed it takes up no space, and when open it faces into the room, offering ample space to hang clothes, stow shoes, and put away an overnight case.

## MAKE IT *yours*

Store out-of-season clothes or seasonal sports equipment in the closet.

Line the closet with cedar, making an upright chest for woolens.

Install shelves for linens.

Set up a pullout craft, hobby, or gift-wrapping headquarters with shelves for supplies and works in progress.

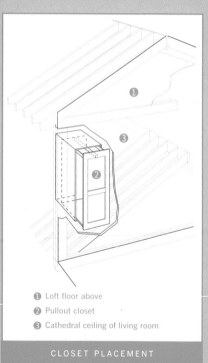

❶ Loft floor above
❷ Pullout closet
❸ Cathedral ceiling of living room

CLOSET PLACEMENT

❶ A REMOVABLE DOWEL is perfect for hanging clothes when needed; it can be taken out to store unwieldy objects.

❷ THE PAINTED cabinet door blends into the wall, all but hiding the closet.

❸ EXCEPT WHEN she has house-guests, the homeowner uses the closet to store art supplies.

# MORE *great* IDEAS

**① THE WALLS** around this tub—a claw-foot unit dropped into a tile-topped tub surround—enfold a luxurious bathing alcove, complete with inset shelves at one end that feature an outlet for a stereo or mood-setting lamp. The wall at the other end has shelves that open to the commode area; these slim shelves are just right for storing toilet paper and other bathroom supplies.

**②** **TAKE ADVANTAGE** of the deep walls surrounding a fireplace to ease storage shortage. These two closets demonstrate numerous options: adjustable shelves, open-front drawers to keep things in view and accessible, half-width and full-width components, extra shelves on the closet doors, and bifold doors where space is especially tight.

**③** **THIS "DRESSER"** is as big as a piece of furniture, yet it's fit entirely within surplus space between wall studs. The clear-finish fir drawers, 18 in. to 20 in. deep, slide into the framed-out knee-wall cavity. Only the ledge above them extends a few inches into the room. Pegs complete the clutter-combating ensemble.

**④** **THE WALL** under this sloped ceiling boxes off a storage bonanza that runs the full length of the room. For versatility and visual relief, open bookcases in the wall cavity are interspersed with cabinets.

**1** INSTEAD OF a chunky medicine cabinet, this sleek bathroom recruits a long, slim strip of wall space to house a shelf covered by clutter-hiding frosted-glass sliders. Notched between wall studs, the adjacent tiled cutout is an airy alcove for soap or incense.

**2** EVEN A SMALL patch of wall space is enough for a bookcase. Dog-eared because of the sloping roof on the other side of the wall, this one is a charmingly quirky nook that keeps favorite books by the bed.

**3** AN ICEMAKER fits under the 12-in.-deep copper countertop of this compact bar by straddling the space between the bar and the powder room on the other side of the 4½-in. wall. The protruding back of the 20-in.-deep icemaker hides under the powder-room vanity top; both countertops are 36 in. high. Water and electrical connections occupy a framing cavity adjacent to the icemaker.

**4** THIS BATHROOM feels bigger than 7½ ft. by 8 ft. because none of the cabinetry occupies floor space. The built-in vanity fills a window niche, and the medicine cabinet tucks between wall studs. With deep shelves at the bottom and shallower ones at the top, the tall cabinet takes full advantage of another between-stud opening under the sloping ceiling.

# SPARE INCHES
## *that count*

some of the most promising untapped spaces are small areas that offer big opportunities for storage solutions.

# *maximizing* KITCHEN STORAGE

This tidy kitchen appears to have a typical assortment of cupboards and drawers, but in fact, the cabinetry is far from typical. Behind the cupboard doors, inside the drawers, and in other cabinets around the kitchen is an intricately planned, highly organized storage system that puts everything in its place, out of view, and still within easy reach.

Wall and base cabinets ring the room, from the breakfast nook at one end to a floor-to-ceiling pantry at the other. The built-in benches in the breakfast nook contain full-length drawers fitted with adjustable dividers for storing bulky items such as lunch boxes and breadbaskets. The pantry looks like a stack of storage cabinets, all the same size. Actually, half of it is 27 in. deep, and the other half, limited by a fireplace behind it, is 12 in. deep. The shallow side houses shelves of staples and a drawer for tall items such as bottles. The deeper side packs in platters and serving pieces along with a pullout shelf for dry goods, another for a television, and a divided drawer big enough for a hefty recycling bin as well as a stash of paper bags. The family message center—a chalkboard—is built into the side panel of the pantry.

➊ **THE DEEP SIDE** of the pantry contains pullout shelves and drawers for a television and food supplies plus a recycling bin with bag storage behind it. The shallow side, in front of the fireplace wall, stows jars, cans, and bottles.

➋ **STORAGE IS OPTIMIZED IN** these understated kitchen cabinets.

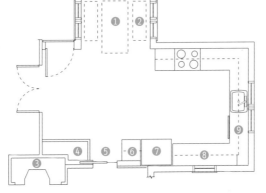

1. BREAKFAST NOOK
2. BENCH SEATS WITH DRAWERS
3. FIREPLACE BEHIND PANTRY WALL
4. PANTRY
5. GLASS-PANELED POCKET DOOR TO LIVING ROOM
6. COOKBOOK SHELVES AND MICROWAVE CABINET
7. REFRIGERATOR
8. BAKING CENTER
9. DISHWASHER BEHIND CABINET FRONT

FLOOR PLAN

**❶** A READY-MADE INSERT makes full use of the space in this corner cabinet. Called a blind corner base system, the hinged insert includes two sets of racks that tuck into the cabinet side by side; when the one attached to the cabinet front is pulled out, the other one slides into view inside the cabinet.

**❷** IN THE BAKING CENTER, the 32-in.-high granite counter is 4 in. lower than the other counters so that it is a more comfortable height for kneading dough. A well-planned mix of drawers accommodates everything from bowls and pans to spices and mixer attachments.

In most kitchens, things stored in the cabinet over the refrigerator are difficult to reach and awkward to pull from unwieldy stacks. But here vertical dividers keep muffin tins, serving trays, and cutting boards side by side and easily retrievable. Cookbooks line open shelves in an adjacent wall cabinet. Below the shelves, a cabinet with a retractable pop-up door keeps the microwave convenient but off the counter and out of sight when not in use.

The kitchen features a special baking center, with a lower counter, just right for kneading dough, as the cornerstone. Under the counter in the center is a bank of drawers—deep ones for storing measuring cups, mixing bowls, and pans, and others that are the depth of spice jars and incorporate a built-in grid of acrylic dividers for organizing them. To the right is a cabinet with a pullout cutting board and a shelf that provides extra counter space when needed. To the left is a cabinet in a corner, another location notorious for inaccessibility. In this kitchen, the corner cabinet is a metaphor for the efficiency of the entire room: Pull open the cabinet door, and a special hinged rack brings four shelves of baking equipment into reach.

Hinge the bench seats or insert shorter drawers instead of using full-length drawers.

Attach a folding stool to the inside of a cabinet door so small children can reach the sink and adults can reach the top shelves of wall cabinets.

Include a built-in work center with desk, phone, computer, and shelves.

Replace part of a base cabinet with a niche for a pet's bed or food and water bowls, or insert a pet-food station in the toekick area.

❸ THE BREAKFAST NOOK has built-in benches with drawers for kitchen supplies that open into the kitchen. The freestanding table can be pulled out of the nook and used as an extra worksurface when needed.

❹ EXTRA-LONG DRAWERS capture all the storage area under the breakfast nook benches. Dividers keep things organized in drawer compartments, and full-extension glides make every compartment accessible.

# accessories
# CLOSET

Most bedroom closets have little room for accessory shelving, and what little there is soon becomes overstuffed. The owner of this house looked outside the closet and discovered extra inches on an adjacent empty wall that had the makings of a purse and hat cabinet. A full-height cavity inside the wall was big enough to spread out a whole wardrobe of purses and headgear, with every item in view and easily accessible. Some items are arranged on a commercially available slat wall-and-hook system; bulkier purses sit on the cabinet's bottom ledge.

The door that covers the accessories closet looks so much like a panel that the simplicity of the fireplace wall is not compromised. There's not even a door handle; instead, a touch latch operates the door.

Taking the idea one step further, the owner replaced a window at the entry to the master bedroom, freeing up a wall for a shoe closet. The 13-in.-wide space houses a floor-to-ceiling cabinet with a dozen adjustable shelves. Each shelf is angled and has a lip at the edge to keep the shoes from slipping off.

The cabinet doors were designed strategically here, too. Since the shoe closet is adjacent to a stairway, it has double doors, rather than a broad single door, that won't obstruct foot traffic.

**❶ ADJUSTABLE SHELVES** fit shoes of all sizes, from boots to sandals.

## MAKE IT *yours*

Create an accessory cabinet on any size wall. Use shelves or hooks for a scarf or jewelry cabinet; install dowels for belts or ties.

And hooks to the closet's shallow side walls to hang belts, necklaces, or sunglasses.

Space permitting, attach a shoe or purse rack to the back of a closet door.

❷ PURSES AND HATS hang two or more deep on long rods, multiplying the closet capacity yet keeping everything in view.

❸ THE DOOR BLENDS seamlessly into the fireplace wall since it was cut from the wall panel.

❹ MOVABLE HOOKS in the purse closet rest securely between slat rails.

# KITCHEN STORAGE
*in a column*

Don't write off columns when scouring a room for storage space. Columns built solely for looks usually are hollow and can be opened up for more productive use. But even structural columns offer storage potential. Both of the columns in this kitchen, one load-bearing and one decorative, house tall cabinets.

A structural column located just in front of the kitchen wall supports the beam that runs above the ovens. The steel column is only 4 in. deep, though, so there was room in front of it for a 12-in.-wide boxed column that continues the lines of the beam and encloses a 5-ft.-tall cabinet. For balance and twice the storage benefit, a look-alike cabinet was built in a column by the refrigerator.

A cabinet company made these slim units to precise specifications so that they appear to be continuations of the columns. Each cabinet is a full 12 in. deep and contains four adjustable shelves. The hinged inset doors match those on the other kitchen cabinets. Both narrow cabinets open toward the center of the kitchen for widest access and are fine places to keep cooking oils, spices, tea, and coffee as well as cookbooks, oven mitts, measuring cups, and small appliances.

**①**

**① JUST A FOOT** wide but 5 ft. tall and 2 ft. deep, these cabinets offer substantial storage space.

**② THE WHITE** column cabinets blend smoothly into the white-painted kitchen. Crown molding ties the kitchen together and gives the tall cabinets the look of furniture pieces.

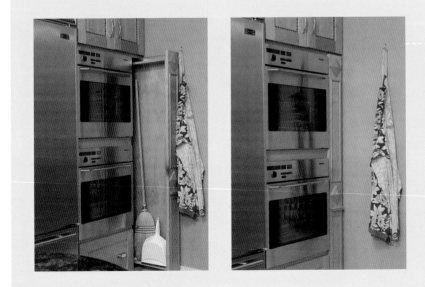

## MAKE IT *yours*

Outfit a tall, narrow space as a broom closet by inserting a drawer sideways. This one is mounted on extra-long drawer glides and has a recessed finger grip on the front so no hardware is needed.

Compartmentalize the cabinet, installing shelves at top and bottom as well as a side-access appliance garage or side-access cookbook shelves.

Locate a short column adjacent to the oven and outfit it with slim drawers or pullout shelves for spices.

Elsewhere in the house, incorporate an outlet and use the cabinet as headquarters for an iron and ironing board.

# BATHROOM
## *storage center*

Even a small master bathroom can provide luxury and comfort. This compact, odd-shaped room pampers the homeowners with a wealth of pleasing features. Instead of a broad, monolithic vanity with twin sinks, they opted for a slim-lined freestanding sink on each side of the room. Complementing "her" sink is a cozy dressing table that is remarkably well stocked.

Along with standard drawers, the furniture-style vanity keeps makeup well organized and accessible in desktop cubby drawers and two narrow under-counter pullouts. A bank of unobtrusive cabinetry runs from the countertop to the ceiling, storing towels, soap, and shampoo. Next to the vanity is a wall-mounted television.

On the other side of the bathroom is a cabinet that, like the vanity, is painted to evoke antique furniture. Inside is more storage space plus a refrigerator and a microwave. A gap between the cabinet and shower is transformed from awkward to elegant by the insertion of glass shelves for towels and display jars. The little cupboard under those shelves completes this picture of comfort and ease. Nestled inside are a coffee maker and all the makings to start the morning off right.

## MAKE IT *yours*

Partner the vanity with a small drop-in sink.

Wire wall cabinets or niches to receive a small stereo system or speakers.

Augment the coffee bar with a mini refrigerator.

Install a pull-out tray under the vanity for a laptop.

**❶ THE ELEGANT VANITY** is finished to look like a fine old desk. In fact, the homeowner sometimes sits here with her laptop.

**❷ A DIVERSE MIX** of drawers, vertical pullouts, cubbies, and wall units makes full use of the available storage space and keeps everything close at hand.

**❸ GLASS SHELVES** dress up the niche by the shower; the coffee cupboard fits flush with the wall.

**❹ BIFOLD DOORS** fold against the wall and out of the way when the coffee cabinet is open. The coffee machine plugs into an outlet inside the cabinet.

# SHALLOW PANTRY
## *on a wall*

*Odd turns and indentations in the walls of older homes add character but they also can add function and style. A jog in the wall of this kitchen presented the homeowners with the perfect space for a pantry, albeit shallow. Adding a sliding door meant the pantry could be opened without blocking traffic in the kitchen.*

What the 5-in. recess lacked in depth it had in breadth, running from floor to ceiling and stretching 44 in. across the wall. The space sports 10 adjustable shelves that store everything from canned goods and spices to linens and glassware.

The homeowners found an old horse stall door at an antique store, scrubbed it down and applied clear shellac. When it's pulled across the pantry, the door hides the utilitarian items on the lower shelves but allows more showy items on the upper shelves to shine through the latticework. Even when it's pulled across the adjacent wall to open the pantry, this handsome old door is a showpiece.

❶

❶ **BEFORE THE SHELVES** were added, this section of wall was blank. It was too shallow for standard shelves, and so close to the kitchen island that standard cabinets would have been in the way.

❷ **TO MAKE FULL USE** of the space, the shelves are positioned to fit items of different sizes.

❸ **DECORATIVE ITEMS** are placed on upper shelves, where they are visible through the latticework. Staples are housed on shelves hidden behind the door.

## MAKE IT *yours*

Remove the hardware from extra doors in your house or other doors that match the house style and retrofit them as sliding doors.

Attach corkboard or a blackboard to make a message center on the sliding door—or simply paint part of the door with chalkboard paint.

Allocate separate storage sections along the wall for food items, cleaning supplies, and other necessities. Install hooks and hangers for brooms and mops.

Create a display area on the shelves and use an old window instead of a door as a sliding panel.

# *under-sink* STORAGE DRAWERS

*The cabinet under the kitchen sink is so convenient—and so useless. But you don't have to move the pipes completely out of the way in order to capitalize on the storage space.*

**❸**

**❶ THE READY-MADE** under-sink unit matches the rest of the kitchen cabinetry in style and proportions. Pipes occupy the top-drawer space, though, so the fronts for those drawers were installed as stationary panels.

**❷ INSTEAD OF EXTENDING** several inches straight down from the drain, the pipes in this assembly come down just 2 in. before running to the back of the cabinet opening.

**❸ TWO LARGE DRAWERS** fit nicely once the pipes were routed to the back of the cabinet space.

The cabinet under the sink in this kitchen was 24 in. from front to back and a robust 36 in. wide. Rerouting the pipes opened up room for two drawers, each 22 in. from front to back and 12 in. deep. A ready-made beech cabinet that matches the rest of the kitchen cabinetry slipped right into the standard cabinet opening; the face panel for the side-by-side top drawers was adapted to become a false front.

Behind that false front is a short pipe that replaces the more typical long ones. A direct connect elbow just 2 in. down from the sink routes the pipes toward the back wall, and extended pipes push the trap all the way to the rear of the cabinet, clearing the way for the drawers. The bottom drawer stores canned goods, while the top drawer holds extra serving dishes and miscellaneous items.

## MAKE IT *yours*

Keep the under-sink area clear of drawers and doors to make knee room for wheelchair access. Attach a panel to cover the pipes, and build in shelving below.

Create a pullout recycling center, affixing a cabinet front to a platform for assorted bins.

Offset the pipes in a bathroom vanity to free up storage space.

# MORE *great* IDEAS

① **OTHERWISE DEAD SPACE** over the short passageway between living room and library is on loan here as an extra bookcase. A painted plywood box built into an opening as wide as the doorway and almost as deep as the passageway can display large books or prized art objects.

② **TALL CABINETS** enliven this narrow wall, making the doorway seem bigger and more inviting. The cabinets are slim—filling the cavity between wall studs—but that's enough space for a display of colorful collectibles such as these vintage pails.

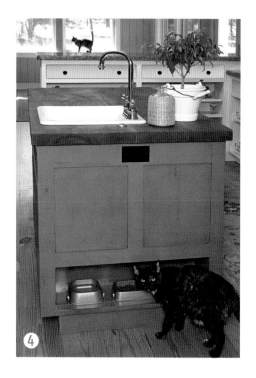

**❸ THE 8-IN. SPACE** between sink and dishwasher in this island houses a versatile, hardworking pullout. The maple butcher block, custom cut to fit the family's knife set, is convenient to the food prep counter; the stainless-steel rods hold dish towels; and the base shelf can store both cooking oils and dish soap.

**❹ THE LOW LEDGE** in this kitchen island is the cat's meow; it keeps the cats' food and water bowls out of the way, yet at 5 in. high, it is easily accessible for the cats. Like a souped-up cookbook shelf, the ledge has a removable acrylic liner for easy cleaning; a small lip on the liner keeps food from falling on the floor.

**❺ ALLOCATING SPACE** for multiple functions is not an either-or process here. With the hinged, solid-surface leaf down and the cabinet door closed, this sunny corner features a sleek counter that stretches over a trash can niche; when the corner is opened up, deep drawers surface, as does a door-mounted magnetic rack for oversized cooking tools.

**❻ THE LEFTOVER CORNER** under the kitchen cabinet is just the spot for parking appliances. This 12-in.-wide, 18-in.-high, 12-in.-deep appliance garage is flush with the countertop so the toaster can slide right out; the door, a mini version of the cabinet doors, blends in for a clean, uncluttered effect.

① SINCE THERE IS NO LIP at the base of these cabinets, suitcases slide out easily and don't have to be lifted out. A light tug on the metal pull activates the hydraulic hinges.

② A GEM of an idea, the cabinets flanking this bathroom mirror are no deeper than the mirror itself but roomy enough to hold a jewelry box's worth of earrings. The melamine cabinets are 2 in. deep by 12 in. wide by 30 in. tall; the earrings hang on bands of $1/4$-in. wood.

③ **THE TAP OF A TOE** opens this touch-latched drawer. The cherry front looks like the other toekicks but is attached to the birch drawer box.

④ **BECAUSE A FIREPLACE** is on the other side, there was enough space to recess deep shelves in this bathroom wall and still leave the 6 in. of airspace required around a firebox and flue. This birch plywood linen closet—18 in. deep, 24 in. wide, and 5 ft. tall—tucks away six adjustable shelves plus a toilet-paper roller.

⑤ **FILLING OUT** a corner by the entry, this closet is only 27 in. on a side yet has 16 hooks for coats, bags, and keys, plus a wraparound shelf for hats, gloves, and purses. Crown molding, bead-board side panels, and a flat top make the 7$\frac{1}{2}$-ft.-high closet look like a corner cupboard; the door was salvaged from a remodeling project.

⑥ **LIKE A BIG CLOSET** spread out in narrow slices, these storage sections press assorted shelves and rods against the attic wall, organizing linens, bedding, and the family's out-of-season clothes without bulging into the room. Slender partitions define the storage area and support the closet components.

# NICHES *and nooks*

*Discover secluded corners or alcoves that can add living area to your home.*

# HALLWAY *office* NICHE

When the owner of this condo uncovered a pocket of empty space inside the hallway wall, he put it to work as a little office. A surprising amount of function fits into this tiny space, and the office is easily filed away after hours.

This niche is just 19 in. wide and 27 in. deep, but that's wide enough to hold a computer keyboard and deep enough for a desktop and computer monitor. At 8½ ft. tall, the space accommodates storage above and below the desktop. The monitor sits behind the keyboard on the desktop, the printer occupies an upper shelf, and the CPU and other computer equipment are stashed under the desk. The only thing missing is the chair, and that's pulled from the living room around the corner.

Walls and ceiling were painted to match the hall, and the shelves were edged with ornamental molding that complements the baseboards and picture rails in the condo. The stained oak strip flooring that's used throughout the condo continues into the niche.

When work is complete, the office disappears behind a piano-hinged panel that's a carbon copy of the fixed panel across the hall. There's not even a doorknob; gentle pressure against the panel releases a touch latch.

❶ **THE OFFICE IS HIDDEN** behind a hinged panel that looks like a wall panel between the hallway and the bedroom; because it uses a touch latch, no door handle is needed.

❷ **BASIC SHELVES** hold the essentials, and artwork dresses up the office.

Extend the desktop with a hinged leaf or pullout mechanism.

Space permitting, incorporate a slot for a folding chair.

Use the niche as a kids' computer station or art center.

Leave off the door and set up the nook as a phone booth or message center.

2

# NO-MESS
## *mudroom*

This mudroom is just a few steps down from the kitchen hallway and very visible from it, so the homeowners wanted it to look as neat and formal as the kitchen and the rest of the living area.

A handsome storage unit pressed into place on the mudroom wall keeps the room tidy. The classic pattern of surrounding wainscotting and crown molding continues onto the cabinetry, making the room feel at one with its surroundings, while open niches add color, depth, and visual relief.

This is a "no excuses" mudroom: With an array of large hooks at various heights and a bench that can work as a table or a step, there's no reason for anyone in the family to leave anything on the floor. Cabinet doors keep coats and sports gear under wraps, and boots line up tidily in low cubbies. Cubbies for sports equipment line the opposite wall, convenient but out of view from other rooms.

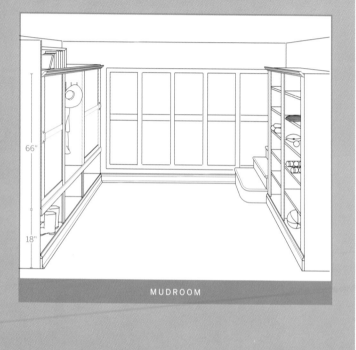

MUDROOM

❶ A COMBINATION of closed and open storage keeps this mudroom neat yet easy to use.

## MAKE IT *yours*

Organize the mudroom with a locker and boot bin for each family member.

Use a slatted base for an umbrella bin and boot cubbies, allowing rain and melting snow to drip into a removable plastic pan underneath.

Cap the everyday storage cabinets with overhead compartments for out-of-season gear.

Include a drawer or two for keys, flashlights, sunglasses, and extra shoelaces.

Add a storage bench with hinged flip tops that can do double-duty.

①

# ATTIC *play* NOOK

Most attics seem smaller than they are due to the low-ceilinged areas. But there often is a lot of space in those low areas, and it can be put to creative use. This attic delights visiting grandchildren, with a light, lofty play area in the center and a snug nook under the eaves.

Wrapped in warm wood paneling, the alcove feels cozy and private. The nautical sconce light at the head of the bed generates ambient light for playtime and over-the-shoulder light for reading in the evening. Sized for a standard twin mattress, the bed nests in a frame atop two deep drawers for toys, books, and pajamas.

Building out the nook a few feet from the corner lines it up with the overhead window and enables it to catch hours of sunlight from the side window. The corner space goes to good use as a closet. True, the sloping roof cuts into the closet area, but there is ample room to hold the few things kids bring along to spend the night at Grandma's.

## MAKE IT *yours*

Build bookshelves into the head or foot of the bed niche.

Cut into the wall to make a secret compartment or cubby with a tiny hinged door.

If the wall is long enough, slip a second bed nook under the eaves. Separate the two beds with a partition; include a pass-through for messages.

Turn the niche into a built-in couch for a rainy-day reading-and-relaxing alcove.

Use the space for a built-in entertainment center. This one, painted in an undersea adventure theme, is as much fun as the toys.

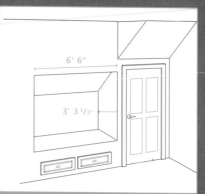

6' 6"

3' 3 1/2"

PLAY NOOK

❶ RESERVE FLOOR AREA by slipping a twin bed under the eaves and creating a reading and sleeping nook for children.

USS·ATTICUS

# LIVING ROOM OFFICE
## *hideaway*

*Put to new use, salvaged architectural parts can transform a space. A reclaimed 19th-century Palladian doorway became the perfect entry for this home office nook built into a loft condo.*

Located in a converted warehouse, the condo had ceilings high enough to embrace the 11-ft.-tall antique. When the historic doors are open, the office is an appealing extension of the living area. When the doors are closed, the door assembly is a dramatic conversation piece.

A new wall built just 17 in. from the wall of the room created a space for the office niche as well as shallow bookcases right and left. Between the bookcases, a deeper bulkhead emerges, featuring the antique doorway in the center. Converted to pocket doors, the old doors retract into the sides of the bulkhead when opened, revealing the desk.

By absorbing the depth of both the bookcases and the bulkhead, the office nook is bigger than it looks—more than 2 ft. deep. Add to that the 7-ft.-plus width of the bulkhead, and the office has room for a desktop, pullout keyboard, monitor and printer shelves, and deep storage shelves on both sides.

❶ THE DOORWAY was stripped down to the last layer of paint and kept in its rough condition for authenticity and raw beauty.

❷ TUCKED INTO the shallow but wide office, keyboard, monitor, and printer fit on roll-out shelves.

## MAKE IT *yours*

Create an office nook without blocking light by enclosing the space with a wall that incorporates a salvaged window.

Make a corner office with an old door on a wall angled across the space.

Use salvaged lumber or old timbers to panel a nook, giving it identity as a separate section of the room it's part of.

②

1. STORAGE DRAWER 10 X 10 IN.
2. PULLOUT STORAGE UNIT 10 X 26 IN.
3. BIN FOR RECORD ALBUMS
4. CD SHELVES $5\frac{1}{2}$ IN. DEEP
5. PULLOUT SHELF FOR STEREO COMPONENTS 20 X 18 IN.
6. PULLOUT SHELF FOR TURNTABLE 20 X 8 IN.
7. STORAGE DRAWER 20 X 6 IN.
8. PULLOUT CD/TAPE STORAGE UNIT, FIVE SHELVES $5\frac{1}{2}$ IN. HIGH, CD SIDE $5\frac{1}{4}$ IN. DEEP, TAPE SIDE $2\frac{1}{2}$ IN. DEEP

**UNDER-STAIRWAY FLOOR PLAN**

# A+ homework
# CENTER

What's the landing place for the children's backpacks at your house? Chances are it's the kitchen counter, the dining-room table, or the floor. Here's a better idea: Carve out a homework station under the stairs. It will get an A+ in most houses. Neither isolated nor in the way, the spot lets adults keep tabs on the kids and, if necessary, help with homework while fixing dinner or doing something else. The kids enjoy the security of being nearby, yet independent.

This homework center takes advantage of space under a stair landing half a flight up. The nook has ample elbow room and a span of wide, high headroom that's a real find under stairs.

Designed like a library carrel, the nook is equipped with an overhead task light, a computer, bookshelves, and a desktop with room for spreading out books or homework. There's space underneath for a backpack. Pencil drawers fit side by side under the desktop, and the three tiers of drawers beneath the stairs can be used for desk supplies or general household storage.

Though it's open to the great room, the study spot is surprisingly conducive to concentration. When she was younger, the homeowners' daughter loved the niche. Now that she's a teenager, she studies in another part of the house, but the nook is used every day as a kitchen office.

❶ DISPLAY SHELVES
❷ INTERIOR SHELF ABOVE DESK
❸ DISPLAY ALCOVE
❹ DRAWERS BELOW STAIRS

DESK PLAN

Build a desk system from stock cabinetry and parts sold at home centers.

Add cubbies for backpacks under the desk.

Make a play station for children, featuring an easy-to-clean laminate countertop. Use the drawers for puzzles, games, and craft supplies.

To help the space stay organized, line the back wall with corkboard or pegboard. Attach small baskets for pencils, paper clips, and note paper.

❶ **THIS HOMEWORK CENTER** under a landing is tall, wide, and essentially rectangular, with lots of usable space. A supporting column is paired with an ornamental one to create display niches.

❷ **DEEP DRAWERS** under the stairs blend into the woodwork. The triangular niche above them adds display space and an open area that highlights the graceful stair angle.

# MORE *great* IDEAS

**❶ THE STEEP CEILING SLOPE** limited usable space in this narrow coat closet. Adding hooks and slim cabinetry tripled its usefulness; coats hang on the back of the door; gift-wrap supplies fill drawers, shelves, and dowels; infrequently needed vacuum-cleaner parts and extension cords are perfect for the drawer farthest back.

**2** A LOW, steeply sloped ceiling and odd-shaped crannies, peculiarities that make this an awkward head-banger of a closet, are exactly what kids love about it as a little playhouse. To delight the imagination and stimulate play, it is inhabited by friendly painted animals and furnished with easy-swing Dutch doors.

**3** DEEP DRAWERS fill this staircase from bottom to top, storing a pantry full of kitchenware. Constructed with heavy-duty full-extension drawer glides and custom-cut cabinet fronts, the drawer units—3 ft. deep, 18 in. wide, and 2 ft. to 4 ft. tall—look like paneling when closed.

**4** THE ROOMY CAVITY under the back stairs makes a convenient dish pantry. It's two steps down from the kitchen, though, so a handled box that matches the kitchen planks levels off the floor when the pantry is closed; the box doubles as an easy-access step stool.

**5** AN UNDER-STAIR RACK avoids a shoe pileup in the entry foyer of this house, where people are asked to remove their shoes. Faced with mahogany to match the staircase, the pullout has two angled tiers and is 1 ft. deep, about $2^3/4$ ft. wide, and 2 ft. tall at the back. Space permitting, a pullout bench would give this shoe station an added lift.

**6** THE STEEPLY SLOPED under-stair ceiling gives this tiny nook—$3^1/3$ ft. deep and less than 5 ft. wide—the headroom and ambience to work as a cozy office off the kitchen. An L-shaped desk and inset shelves maximize work and storage space; the stock wood cabinets and solid-surface desktop match materials used in the kitchen.

**7** STAIR, SEAT, and mitten storage are rolled into one here, stepping up the usefulness of the entry area in a smooth, streamlined way. The second step is 15 in. off the floor, just right for a bench; it wraps around the corner to form a 20-in.-deep seat with a matching Brazilian cherry piano-hinged top.

143

# *expandable* ROOMS

Multiply the use and impact of available space by introducing creative dividers, wall cutouts, and other imaginative devices.

# BATHROOM
## *reconfigured*

Small bathrooms can present big problems. There's so little room to work with and so much to fit in—tub, sink, and toilet, not to mention countertops and assorted storage. This decades-old bathroom had chunks bitten off for a hall closet and an angled entry, reducing it to a skimpy 6 ft. by 10 ft. The layout made it feel smaller still, with a sprawling built-in tub-shower unit and squandered floor space in the corner behind the closet wall.

Smart changes eliminated all those problems. First the homeowners removed the hall closet, bumped out the bathroom wall to absorb the closet space, and squared off the entry. Then they pulled out the hulking tub-shower unit and an inconvenient bathroom closet across from it. Those few changes created a 10-ft. by 10-ft. bathroom with uninterrupted floor space awash in light from the bathroom window.

To replace the hall closet and a couple of inadequate bathroom cabinets, the homeowners brought in a tall ready-made unit that bundles linens and bathroom supplies in one place. Toiletries are stashed in a medicine cabinet that hides behind a wood-framed mirror over the sink and in a hidden drawer under the sink.

**① BEFORE** The existing bathroom was dark and dull. Both the bulky tub-shower unit and the closet across from it bulged out from the wall, hogging floor space.

**❷ STYLISH IN APPEARANCE** and space saving in placement, the freestanding round shower, compact vanity table with basin sink, and elegant oval bathtub are arranged around the room to preserve central floor space and share sunlight from the window.

All the fixtures and furnishings in the room are freestanding to conserve floor area and add style. The contemporary basin-style unit appears to perch like an old-fashioned washbowl on a compact table. The lines of the basin are echoed in the sleek oval tub, which is big enough to accommodate two people but whose narrow base makes it seem smaller.

The bathroom has room for a separate shower now, but the homeowners eschewed a typical boxy corner unit, worried that it would compromise the openness of the room. Instead, they installed the freestanding round shower, which takes less space. The shower stall looks airy and weightless, and the ceiling-mounted showerhead makes every shower feel as refreshing as spring rain.

## MAKE IT *yours*

To conserve space but incorporate a vanity top, install a small vanity with a drop-in sink or a pedestal sink with a small adjacent cabinet.

Instead of a freestanding tub, choose a compact corner unit.

Utilize space between wall studs for shallow recessed cabinets or shelves in the shower-tub area or the main area of the bathroom. Paint the cabinet doors the color of the walls so they blend in.

Use a frosted, fluted, or light-colored stained-glass partition to give the toilet area privacy without blocking light.

❶ THE SLIM, tall ready-made closet consolidates linens and bath supplies inside the room in a place where it doesn't block traffic. Tucked into a notch in the wall, it looks like a built-in. The toilet has been rotated to free up this wall.

❷ A CHANGING DISPLAY of artwork hangs from the picture rail that rings the room and ties it together. The sculptural tub with striking-looking faucet is a work of art in itself; the refurbished piano bench can be used as a seat or a table.

②

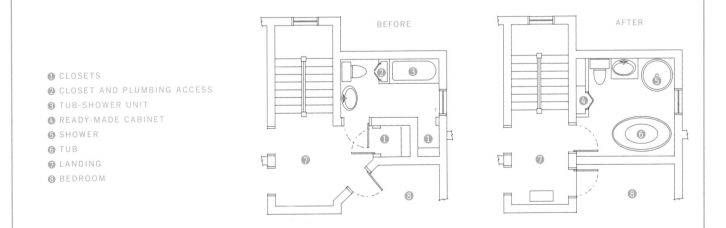

BEFORE

AFTER

1 CLOSETS
2 CLOSET AND PLUMBING ACCESS
3 TUB-SHOWER UNIT
4 READY-MADE CABINET
5 SHOWER
6 TUB
7 LANDING
8 BEDROOM

FLOOR PLANS

# SHARED OFFICE
## *and nursery*

*Unless you have a spare bedroom, the arrival of a new baby may mean the demise of your much-needed study or home office. But the computer still has to go someplace. This homeowner devised a way for baby and business to share a room and still have space of their own.*

The second-floor office was relatively large, but sloped ceilings at both ends cut deeply into the usable space. A narrow closet hugged the wall under one low ceiling, but the rest of the space in the soon-to-be nursery was undefined. By adding an interior wall where the ceiling begins to slope at one end of the room, the homeowner effectively eliminated one low-ceilinged area from the main room and divided the room into three parts. The main room became the nursery. Behind the new wall are a walk-in closet and a small but efficient home office. Cabinets and bookcases line the new wall on the nursery side. The low bookshelves are stocked with children's books, and the higher ones hold reference books that are handy just outside the homeowner's office. Diapers and other baby-care essentials are kept in the base cabinets.

**❶ BEFORE** This second-story home office contained a haphazard array of furniture. The space under the sloped ceilings was underused or left empty.

**❷ WELL-PLACED BUILT-INS** and interior walls organize the room into an attractive, multifunctional space. The bureau and changing table, under-bed drawers, base cabinets, and closet are great for the child; high shelves display collectibles and keep reference books handy just outside Mom's office.

The new closet rendered the old one unnecessary. In its place, the homeowner created a cozy bed alcove with a built-in twin bed platform atop jumbo drawers. A low partition forms one end of the alcove.

The partition tees into an existing wall that covers a protruding air-handling chase. Removing the wall wasn't possible, but extending it about a foot turned it into an asset. The wall makes a perfect place for a built-in bureau with removable changing table. And because the wall is now 6 in. wider than the bureau, there's room behind it for two bonuses—a lighted display niche or bedside shelf in the bed alcove, and a nook by the room entry with a low shelf and coat hooks just right for a toddler to use all by himself. For now, the crib sits in a sheltered corner. When no longer needed, it will be removed to open up more play space.

❶ THE OFFICE, the size of a walk-in closet, is equipped with a built-in desktop, file cabinets, and computer. It's a quiet place for Mom to work, but close to the nursery so she can keep an eye on the baby.

❷ BEHIND THE CHANGING STATION, a short wall carves out a changing station of sorts for the little boy; furnished with a low shelf and kid-height hooks, it's a good place for a toddler to hang his pajamas or find the clothes that have been picked out for the day.

❸ A BUILT-IN twin-size bed platform with integrated drawers nestles into a deep alcove under one of the sloping ceilings. The lighted wall niche is a display space now and will be a handy bedside bookshelf when the baby graduates from the crib to this bed.

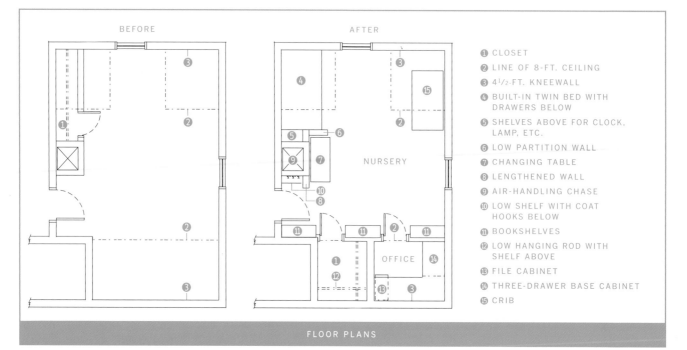

**BEFORE**

**AFTER**

NURSERY

OFFICE

❶ CLOSET
❷ LINE OF 8-FT. CEILING
❸ 4½-FT. KNEEWALL
❹ BUILT-IN TWIN BED WITH DRAWERS BELOW
❺ SHELVES ABOVE FOR CLOCK, LAMP, ETC.
❻ LOW PARTITION WALL
❼ CHANGING TABLE
❽ LENGTHENED WALL
❾ AIR-HANDLING CHASE
❿ LOW SHELF WITH COAT HOOKS BELOW
⓫ BOOKSHELVES
⓬ LOW HANGING ROD WITH SHELF ABOVE
⓭ FILE CABINET
⓮ THREE-DRAWER BASE CABINET
⓯ CRIB

**FLOOR PLANS**

## MAKE IT *yours*

Run a toy shelf along a low wall under the sloping ceiling. Under the shelf, park toy bins mounted on casters; loaded with blocks and LEGO® pieces, the bins can be rolled out for play, then easily put away.

Instead of an office, use the space as a play area. Replace the door with curtains or a half-height door, and furnish the room with a little chair, a few shelves, and a soft carpet. Wire the room for eventual conversion to a computer zone.

Install a half-height door with short curtains above, and turn the closet into a puppet theater. Insert a trundle bed under the bed instead of drawers or, space permitting, under them.

If the ceiling is high enough, insert double bunks in the bed niche.

To make room for twins, build a bed platform and drawers on each side of the room. Instead of a closet-office combo, build side-by-side closets.

③

②

153

# CREATIVE ATTIC
## *play space*

Even if they are overflowing with great toys, playrooms are no fun if the rooms themselves are boring. The best playrooms are bright, dynamic spaces organized with kid-size play centers that offer a stimulating choice of age-appropriate activities. This attic playroom for two small girls used to be dark and dull, nothing more than a bland space cluttered with a jumble of toys. Now it is a play paradise.

The floor area is wide open for active play, and the vibrantly painted walls are ringed with well-spaced play stations. One of the highlights is a shingle-roofed playhouse built against one wall and furnished as an art center. A wall-mounted lamp illuminates the art space, and a sheet of vinyl flooring protects the carpet from spills. Chalkboard "windows" turn the outside of the house's plywood walls into art areas, too.

Two closets under the eaves have been trans-formed into inspired kids' spaces. Interior windows were cut into the interior wall of each. An aquarium fills the opening in one; the other is set up as a puppet theater stage. A curtain of vinyl "seaweed" streamers replaces the door of the aquarium closet. To expand play possibilities, the door to the theater closet was cut and rehung as a half door. Both closet interiors were carpeted, colorfully painted, and furnished with a built-in bench and a wall lamp so they can double as clubhouses or cozy nap spots.

The window bay across the room became a dress-up place with whimsical pegs, a mirror at child's height, and a half door shaped like a cloud.

❶

❶ **WHIMSICAL DETAILS** such as this wall peg in the dress-up area take advantage of every opportunity to make the room fun and fanciful.

❷ **OPEN SHELVES** and jumbo drawers store toys under the eaves. A cloud-shaped gate turns the window alcove into an enticing area for dress-up or imaginative play. Though set up as an arts-and-crafts station, the house can be adapted for other make-believe play, too.

## MAKE IT *yours*

Install a chalkboard in one exterior "window" of the art house and hang a roll or pad of art paper in the other. Put grass-green vinyl sheet flooring around the outside of the house to enhance the effect and to shield the carpet from paint and chalk dust.

Design the house as a reading hut or game station with soft cushions, a book rack, and a game table.

Instead of a house, decorate the structure to look like a car or bus, with cutout windows, an operable steering wheel, and a dashboard with movable parts.

Cover the outside walls of the puppet theater with chalkboard paint or magnetic paint so the space can be reinvented as a store, clubhouse, train, or sheriff's office.

If there is no closet or other potential playhouse structure under the eaves, build a wall to define a play zone. Use cutout "windows" and "doors" to enliven the space with light and views.

155

A play kitchen with a portable table fills another corner of the room. When they are in the mood for active play, the girls can scramble up the wall-mounted climbing ladder or skip across the canvas hopscotch pad. When they want to read, they can choose a book from the bookcase placed in front of the aquarium.

Even the toy storage is part of the fun now. A hinged-top bench built into the sunny dormer between closets functions as a window seat and toy box. Games are stored in a cabinet "tower" adjacent to the aquarium. More toys are stowed in existing attic drawers that, freshly painted in bright colors, beckon children to discover the surprises inside.

❸ LIKE A MAGICAL PICTURE over the bookcase, a
30-gallon aquarium fills the cutout in this closet wall. Even
with the fish tank supports inside, there's room to play in the
closet; a "seaweed" curtain enhances the marine fantasy. In
front of the closet, a two-tiered cabinet stores games.

❹ COLORFUL PAINT enlivens the playroom and visually
smoothes out the dips and turns of the walls. A half door
and a window cutout transform a stuffy attic closet into a
puppet theater.

# *entry*
# COMMAND CENTRAL

The most-used path in and out of many houses is the ugliest and most neglected—the route through the back door. Coming in from the garage, the family in this house used to trek through a small, overstuffed mudroom/laundry room before they reached their nice kitchen. They wanted a back entrance that looked better, separated functions more cleanly, and provided more storage.

They also wanted a home office near the kitchen so that Mom would no longer be relegated to a patch of kitchen counter or a tiny table in the corner of the bedroom.

Handsome freestanding cabinetry helped make both wishes a reality. A small addition allowed the homeowners to separate the laundry from the mudroom, so that the garage door opened directly into a mudroom/foyer. What's most remarkable, though, is the magic worked by the cabinet structure in the foyer. The 7-ft.-tall unit acts like a wall, framing the foyer space and furnishing it with an impressive inventory of cabinets and cubbies. Shaped like an L, the back of the cabinetry sculpts an office zone just outside the kitchen. Here the unit is outfitted with file drawers, cubbies for books, and a long wraparound desk. The end cabinet stows office supplies and a printer.

The office and foyer space is just 10 ft. by 14 ft., but dividing it with the cabinet partition makes it so efficient and dynamic that it feels big. Tile flooring unites the area, and a lofty, skylighted ceiling makes the space bright, airy, and upbeat.

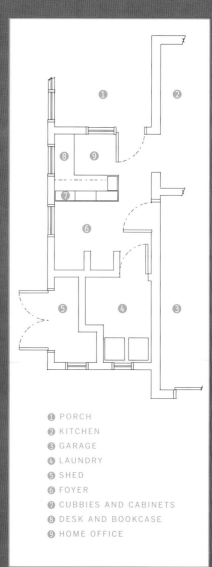

1 PORCH
2 KITCHEN
3 GARAGE
4 LAUNDRY
5 SHED
6 FOYER
7 CUBBIES AND CABINETS
8 DESK AND BOOKCASE
9 HOME OFFICE

FLOOR PLAN

# MAKE IT *yours*

Put a two-sided cabinet partition by the front door to define the entry and create a hall closet. Fill the other side of the cabinet with cupboards and display shelves.

In a child's room, build a partition with a desk and shelves on one side. Use the other as a headboard with an integrated bookshelf.

Assemble stackable modular furniture to make a low partition that defines and organizes the entry foyer or any living space. A partition 2 ft. to 3 ft. tall can provide a tabletop surface as well as storage.

❶ THE EXTRA-DEEP end-cabinet area delineates and shelters the office space, giving it some privacy. In the foyer, jackets hang on high and low rods in neat, accessible wall niches; above them are niches for displaying artwork.

❷ THE WALL of cabinets is tall enough to define the foyer area without blocking light from the high window. Large cabinets punctuated by double rows of cubbies provide ample storage and a vibrant, colorful look.

# *beyond*
# THE BASIC COUCH

Open living/dining areas offer a home a sense of expansiveness, long views, and shared light. Without some definition, though, they can feel amorphous and uninviting. Even an exhilaratingly open space needs some delineation of function as long as the dividers are short enough to preserve open circulation between spaces and low enough to allow conversation and visual contact across borders. Soft boundary markers—that is, devices that shape spaces without sealing them off—actually make open living areas more appealing and more usable.

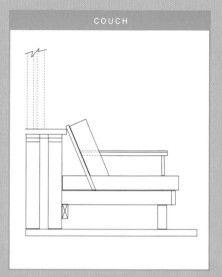

COUCH

In this house, a triple-duty built-in spans the boundary between dining and living areas, defining both areas without cramping the style of the open plan. On the dining side, the broad back of the structure works as a sideboard and as a cabinet to display the family's fine china. On the other side, the built-in forms a hospitable seating ell with a library alcove beyond.

Each arm of the seating ell contains a comfy couch, complete with integral armrest. And when guests spend the night, the ell transforms with ease into a sleeping area—each couch seat is a twin-size bed. The couch back cushions are bolsters against wood frames. Angled for seat-back comfort and positioned at the right depth for a couch seat, the frames pull out to expose the full depth of the mattresses. The enfolding walls of the ell are high enough to scribe a sheltered sleeping area yet low enough to admit a wash of morning sun.

## MAKE IT *yours*

Instead of china cabinets, line the back of the ell with solid cabinet doors, bookshelves, or a combination of the two.

To establish a sitting area outside the structure and enclose a library furnished with freestanding chairs, turn the system inside out, placing built-in seating on the outside and cabinetry around the enclosed space.

Insert display shelves on the side panel of the couch partition to smooth the transition from area to area.

Use the room divider idea in a teenager's room, creating a sleeping alcove on the inside and storage around the outside. Deepen the countertop and eliminate a base cabinet to make a desk in one corner.

❶ THE COUCHES are ready-made beds; all you have to do is remove the backs and cushions. A low ledge runs continuously around the living room and library, defining a large, open area that frames the more intimate spaces.

❷ EVEN WHEN SEATED at the dining table, the homeowners can see and chat with people in other parts of the room.

# reconnected
# KITCHEN

*Before it was liberated from its confining walls, the kitchen in this small house was dark and isolated—except for the traffic routed through it by an ill-conceived hall. A skimpy pass-through on the dining room side was little more than a peephole. Around the corner, a solid wall between kitchen and family room blocked social interchange entirely. Removing both kitchen walls would have created more problems, overexposing the kitchen and eroding the organization of spaces. Removing part of a wall? Adding a half wall? Now, that's a different story.*

**❶ BEFORE** Interior walls chopped the living space into small, dark compartments. A skimpy window did little to connect the dining room and kitchen; the wall between kitchen and family room precluded any connection.

One wall—between the kitchen/hall area and the dining room—came out. It was replaced with a peninsula that was positioned 3 ft. into the dining room to move hallway traffic out of the kitchen. The peninsula preserves the important division between kitchen and dining room. At the same time, the opening above it visually enlarges both rooms and lets conversation flow between them. The granite-topped ledge of the peninsula wall is 12 in. higher than the kitchen counter, to hide food-prep clutter while functioning as a serving surface or buffet.

On the family-room side, a gently arched opening transforms the forbidding wall into a cheery breakfast bar. The granite counter mimics the curve of the archway, forming a gathering place that comfortably seats four.

Though much of the kitchen layout was unchanged, the room is far more efficient. New counters along the open walls more than double the workspace. There's even more storage, thanks to the new cabinets in the peninsula.

The breakfast bar is the new hub of the house. In the kitchen, the homeowner pulls up a stool to work there and get the day's news from her children as they perch at the counter eating their after-school snack. Dinner usually is served at the counter, too. In fact, you might say that the family now has the eat-in kitchen they always wanted.

**❷ WALLS STILL DEFINE** the rooms, but large wall openings connect them visually and make them feel bigger. Matching tones, materials, and light fixtures unify the rooms to enhance the sense of spaciousness.

2

## MAKE IT *yours*

Add shelves or cabinets under the new kitchen counters.

Hang open shelves or glassware racks from the top of the dining room pass-through.

Install china and serving-ware cabinets that have doors on both sides of the peninsula so that they can be opened from both the dining room and the kitchen.

Install recessed or pendant lighting above the peninsula; use a dimmer switch so the lighting can be adjusted for ambience.

Run wiring to the peninsula and the breakfast bar so that you can put a coffee maker, microwave, warming drawer, or icemaker here.

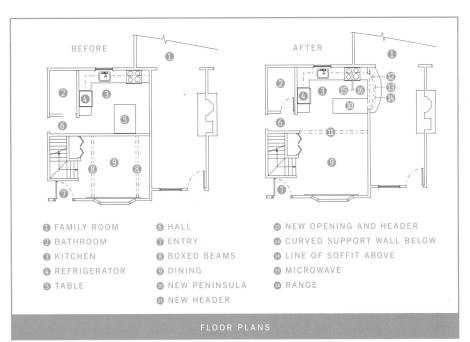

BEFORE

AFTER

① FAMILY ROOM
② BATHROOM
③ KITCHEN
④ REFRIGERATOR
⑤ TABLE

⑥ HALL
⑦ ENTRY
⑧ BOXED BEAMS
⑨ DINING
⑩ NEW PENINSULA
⑪ NEW HEADER

⑫ NEW OPENING AND HEADER
⑬ CURVED SUPPORT WALL BELOW
⑭ LINE OF SOFFIT ABOVE
⑮ MICROWAVE
⑯ RANGE

FLOOR PLANS

# MORE *great* IDEAS

**1** THE CHILDREN in this house have separate bedrooms but shared play space in a 7-ft. by 7-ft. loft. Reached by a ladder in each room, the plywood loft with cork floor and acrylic rails forms a T across the wall, creating a canopy over the beds. A cutout low in the wall works as pass-through and friendly link. A door can be installed for added fun.

**2** SLIDING SHOJI SCREENS open for shared views and blended spaces in this apartment. Even when they're closed for privacy, the screens allow natural light to filter into the bedroom. Made of rice paper and maple, the 3-ft.-wide, $4\frac{1}{2}$-ft.-high screens run in grooves notched into the cabinet/dividing wall.

**3** THIS GUEST ROOM boldly seizes space for a closet and bed loft. Hiding behind the wall is headroom for the basement stairs and, next to it, a closet. Bonus storage in the raised pedestal by the door opens to the closet. Pressed against the wall, the ladder pivots out so kids can climb up to bed.

**4** TAKING ADVANTAGE of the high ceiling, a loft structure expands the square footage and delineates zones in this apartment. The multipurpose "second floor," accessed by a pull-down attic ladder, forms a ceiling that joins with support posts and half walls to define an office in a corner of the living area.

⑤ CONSOLIDATING TWIN BEDS and storage in one multidimensional structure conserves floor space and organizes this small, shared room. Each boy has bedside shelving and an exclusive bulletin board. Drawers and shelves line the back of the structure, and more shelves fit under the bottom bunk. A ship's ladder and pipe railings lend a salty air.

⑥ WITH A STAINED-GLASS window in the wall between them, both the sitting room and the powder room enjoy light and a window as pretty as a picture. Placed high on the wall, the window affords privacy in the powder room but makes the tiny room seem less confining. The room's pocket door conserves floor space.

⑦ BOTH OPENINGS and dividers expand the living space here. A keyhole entry and a pass-through connect the kitchen with the entertainment spaces without sacrificing much cabinet area. Two-sided cabinets between drywall columns define the dining area; light and views flow through the "window" they form, and circulation flows on both sides of the airy partition.

⑧ SOMETIMES YOU NEED an island, sometimes you don't. This granite-topped island, on large casters, tucks under the kitchen counter and functions as a cabinet until it's rolled out to provide an extra worksurface or buffet. The island—20 in. wide, 22 in. deep, and 22 in. high—matches the maple kitchen cabinets.

⑨ OPENWORK WOOD PANELS divide the hallway from the family room without blocking views and light or inhibiting the feeling of open space. The panels pivot to reshape the space, change the circulation pattern, or incorporate the hall area into the family room.

⑨

# PHOTO CREDITS

p. 8: Courtesy Dean Durst; design: Durst Construction, Charlton, NY

p. 9: © Sandy Agrafiotis Photographer; design: Joanne S. Hurd, J.S. Hurd Kitchen & Bath, Gloucester, MA

p. 10: © Phillip Ennis Photography

p. 11: © Jessie Walker

p. 12: © Ken Gutmaker

p. 13: © Ken Gutmaker; design: Susan Thabit, Balboa Island, CA, and Doug Root, Premiere Woodworks, Newport Beach, CA

p. 14: © John Murphy; design: John Murphy, Kingston Springs, TN (top); Ken Vaughn Photography; design: D&D Remodel/Design, Irving, TX (bottom)

p. 15: © Roger Turk/Northlight Photography, Inc.; design: Michael A. Powers, Prestige Builders, Inc., Edmonds, WA

p. 16: © Mark Samu/Samu Studios Inc.; design: Dan Barsanti, Healing Barsanti, Inc., Westport, CT (left); © Anthony Tripp; design: Don Van Cura Construction Co., Chicago, IL (right)

p. 17: © Randy O'Rourke; design: Mark T. White, CKD, Kitchen Encounters, Annapolis, MD, custom carpenter: Dallas Jones

p. 19: Brian Pontolilo, © The Taunton Press, Inc.; design: Gale Goss, AIA, Estes/Twombly Architects, Newport, RI (left); © Sandy Agrafiotis Photographer (top right); © Sam Gray Photography; design: LDa Architects, LLP, Cambridge, MA (bottom right)

p. 20: © Christopher J. Scalise; design: Susan Balk, Pinckney, MI (left); © Ken Gutmaker; design: Deborah Kadas Design, Corvallis, OR, general contractors: JD Construction and Bridgetown Construction, Corvallis, OR (center); © Chipper Hatter; design: H. Dale Contant, CR, Atlanta Design & Build, Marietta, GA (right)

p. 21: © Seth Tice-Lewis; design and construction: Michael Chandler and Beth Williams, Chandler Design-Build, Chapel Hill, NC (left); © Ken Gutmaker; design: Jeff Talmadge, Talmadge Construction, Inc., Aptos, CA; construction: John Wallis, Wallis Woodworks, Santa Cruz, CA (center); © 2003 Brian Vanden Brink, Photographer; design: John Cole Architect, Arlington, MA, and Fryeburg, ME (right)

p. 22: Courtesy Susan Balk (top); © Christopher J. Scalise; design: Susan Balk, Pinckney, MI (bottom)

p. 23: © Christopher J. Scalise; design: Susan Balk, Pinckney, MI

p. 25–26: © Ken Gutmaker; design: Deborah Kadas Design, Corvallis, OR; general contractors: JD Construction and Bridgetown Construction, Corvallis, OR

p. 27: © Ken Gutmaker; design: Deborah Kadas Design, Corvallis, OR; general contractors: JD Construction and Bridgetown

Construction, Corvallis, OR (left); © Björg Magnea, design: David Varnish Architects, New York, NY (right top and bottom)

p. 28: © Chipper Hatter; design: H. Dale Contant, CR, Atlanta Design & Build, Marietta, GA

p. 29: © Chipper Hatter; design: H. Dale Contant, CR, Atlanta Design & Build, Marietta, GA

p. 30–31: © Seth Tice-Lewis; design and construction: Michael Chandler and Beth Williams, Chandler Design-Build, Chapel Hill, NC

p. 32–33: © Darel Gabriel Bridges; design: Richard Manzo, Knight Associates, Architects, Blue Hill, ME; builder: Duddy & Associates, Sedgwick, ME

p. 35: © Ken Gutmaker; design: Jeff Talmadge, Talmadge Construction, Inc., Aptos, CA; construction: John Wallis, Wallis Woodworks, Santa Cruz, CA

p. 36: © Ken Gutmaker; design: Deborah Kadas Design, Corvallis, OR; general contractor: G. Christianson Construction, Inc., Corvallis, OR

p. 37: © Robert Perron; design: Interdesign Limited, Old Lyme, CT (top left); © 2003 Brian Vanden Brink, Photographer; design: John Cole Architect, Arlington, MA, and Fryeburg, ME (top right); © 2005 Brian Vanden Brink, Photographer; design: John Cole Architect, Arlington, MA, and Fryeburg, ME (bottom)

p. 38: © Tim Street-Porter (top left); © 2005 Brian Vanden Brink, Photographer; design: John Cole Architect, Arlington, MA, and Fryeburg, ME (top right); © Seth Tice-Lewis; design and construction: Michael Chandler and Beth Williams, Chandler Design-Build, Chapel Hill, NC (bottom left and right)

p. 39: © Ken Gutmaker; design: Deborah Kadas Design, Corvallis, OR; general contractor: TL Waterman, Corvallis, OR

p. 40: © Ken Gutmaker; design: Deborah Kadas Design, Corvallis, OR; general contractor: JD Construction, Corvallis, OR (left); © Ken Gutmaker; design: Deborah Kadas Design, Corvallis, OR; general contractor: JD Construction, Corvallis, OR (center); © Ken Gutmaker; design: Susan Thabit, Balboa Island, CA, Christine Fink, Christine Fink Interior Design, Laguna Beach, CA, Doug Root, Premiere Woodworks, Newport Beach, CA (right)

p. 41: © Ken Gutmaker; design: Susan Thabit, Balboa Island, CA, Christine Fink, Christine Fink Interior Design, Laguna Beach, CA, Doug Root, Premiere Woodworks, Newport Beach, CA (left); © Mark Samu/Samu Studios Inc.; design: Lucianna Samu (center); © Chipper Hatter; design: Jay A. Waronker, Architect, Atlanta, GA (right)

p. 42–45: © Ken Gutmaker; design: Deborah Kadas Design, Corvallis, OR; general contractor: JD Construction, Corvallis, OR

p. 46–47: © Ken Gutmaker; design: Susan Thabit, Balboa Island, CA, Christine Fink, Christine Fink Interior Design, Laguna Beach, CA, Doug Root, Premiere Woodworks, Newport Beach, CA

p. 48: © Peter Krupenye; design: The Office of Carol J. W. Kurth, AIA Architect, PC, Bedford, NY

p. 49: © Peter Krupenye; design: The Office of Carol J. W. Kurth, AIA Architect, PC, Bedford, NY (top); © Mark Samu/Samu Studios Inc., design: Jean Stoffer Design, River Forest, IL (bottom left and right)

p. 51: © Ken Gutmaker; design: Susan Thabit, Balboa Island, CA, Christine Fink, Christine Fink Interior Design, Laguna Beach, CA, Doug Root, Premiere Woodworks, Newport Beach, CA

p. 52: © Mark Samu/Samu Studios Inc.

p. 53: © Mark Samu/Samu Studios Inc.; design: Lucianna Samu

p. 54–55: © Seth Tice-Lewis; design and construction: Michael Chandler and Beth Williams, Chandler Design-Build, Chapel Hill, NC

p. 56: © Chipper Hatter; design: Jay A. Waronker, Architect, Atlanta, GA (left); © Philip Clayton-Thompson Photography; styling by Donna Pizzi (right)

p. 57: Mark Peters; design: Moore Construction, Oakdale, CA (top left); © Chandler Photography; design: LeAnne Roberts Designs, Bend, OR (top center); © Mark Samu/Samu Studios Inc.; design: Rick Shaver, Shaver/Melahn Studios, New York, NY (top right); © 2000 Brian Vanden Brink, Photographer; design: Sally Weston Associates, Hingham, MA (bottom)

p. 58: © Roger Turk, Northlight Photography; design: Crafted Interiors, Seattle, WA (top right); © Lee Brauer; design: Grace Street Residential Design Systems, Richmond, VA (left and bottom right)

p. 59: Mark Peters; design: Moore Construction, Oakdale, CA (top); © Chipper Hatter; design: H. Dale Contant, CR, Atlanta Design & Build, Marietta, GA (bottom left); © Randy O'Rourke; design: Mark T. White, CKD, Kitchen Encounters, Annapolis, MD (bottom center); © Sandy Agrafiotis (bottom right)

p. 60: © Chipper Hatter; design: Jay A. Waronker, architect, Atlanta, GA (left); © Peter Vanderwarker Photographs; design: Treff LaFleche, LDA Architects, LLP, Cambridge, MA; construction: Russ Macomber, Macomber Carpentry and Construction, Tewksbury, MA (center); © Susan Gilmore; design: Murphy Bros. Designers & Remodelers, Twin Cities, MN (right)

p. 61: © Anne Gummerson Photography, design: William L. Lupton, Bay City Builders, Inc., Baltimore, MD (left); © Barry Halkin Architectural Photography; design and construction: Marian Tlush Barton and Craig Barton (center); © Susan Gilmore; design: Murphy Bros. Designers & Remodelers, Twin Cities, MN (right)

p. 62–63: © Chipper Hatter; design: Jay A. Waronker, architect, Atlanta, GA

p. 65: © Peter Vanderwarker Photographs; design: Tress LaFleche, LDa Architects, LLP, Cambridge, MA; construction: Russ Macomber, Macomber Carpentry and Construction, Tewksbury, MA (left); © Susan Gilmore; design: Orfield Design & Construction, Inc., Edina, MN (right)

p. 66: © Ken Gutmaker; design: Susan Thabit, Balboa Island, CA, and Doug Root, Premiere Woodworks, Newport Beach, CA; mural by Rick Butcher

p. 67: © 2004 Brian Vanden Brink, Photographer; design: Barba + Wheelock Architecture, Preservation + Design, Portland, ME

p. 68–69: © Anne Gummerson Photography; design: William L. Lupton, Bay City Builders, Inc., Baltimore, MD

p. 70: © Barry Halkin Architectural Photography; design and construction: Marian Tlush Barton and Craig Barton

p. 71: © Barry Halkin Architectural Photography; design and construction: Marian Tlush Barton and Craig Barton (left); © Carolyn L. Bates; design: Thomas D. Cabot AIA, Shelburne, VT (right)

p. 72: Courtesy Murphy Bros. Designers & Builders

p. 73: © Susan Gilmore; design: Murphy Bros. Designers & Builders, Twin Cities, MN

p. 74: © Seth Tice-Lewis; design and construction: Michael Chandler, Chandler Design-Build, Chapel Hill, NC (left and center); © Roger Turk/Northlight Photography; design: Nia Collins, ASID, Collins Group Design & Architecture, Seattle, WA

p. 75: © Robert Perron; design: Architect Robert Orr with architect Melanie Taylor, New Haven, CT (left); © Sandy Agrafiotis Photographer; design: Benjamin Nutter Associates Architects, Topsfield, MA (right)

p. 76: © Randy O'Rourke; design: Chuck Green, Four Corners, Ashland, MA (left); © Ken Gutmaker (right)

p. 77: ©Phillip Ennis Photography; design: Blodgett Designs (left); © Roger Turk/ Northlight Photography; design: Matt Pyka, Pacific Crest Cabinets (right)

p. 78: © Greg Premru; design: Leslie Saul and Associates, Cambridge, MA (left); © Lee Brauer; design: Grace Street Residential

Design Systems, Richmond, VA (center); © 2004 Brian Vanden Brink, Photographer; design: Lisa Ekus-Saffer, Hatfield, MA, construction: Henry Walas, Walas Contracting, Belchertown, MA (right)

p. 79: © Roger Hardy; design: Linder Jones, Harrell Remodeling, Inc., Mountain View, CA (left); © Alise O'Brien Photography; design: Barbara Slavkin, Allied Member, ASID, June Roesslein Interiors, Chesterfield, MO (center); © 2003 Sylvia Martin Photographer; design: Mike McKay, CGR, CAPS, Oak Alley, Inc., Birmingham, AL (right)

p. 81: © Greg Premru; design: Leslie Saul and Associates, Cambridge, MA

p. 82–83: © Lee Brauer; design: Grace Street Residential Design Systems, Richmond, VA

p. 84: © 2004 Brian Vanden Brink, Photographer; design: Lisa Ekus-Saffer, Hatfield, MA; construction: Henry Walas, Walas Contracting, Belchertown, MA

p. 85: © 2004 Brian Vanden Brink, Photographer; design: Lisa Ekus-Saffer, Hatfield, MA; construction: Henry Walas, Walas Contracting, Belchertown, MA (left); © Paul Schlismann; design: de Giulio kitchen design; Wilmette and Chicago, IL (right)

p. 86–87: © Roger Hardy; design: Linder Jones, Harrell Remodeling, Inc., Mountain View, CA

p. 88: Courtesy Barbara Slavkin (top); © Alise O'Brien Photography; design: Barbara Slavkin, Allied Member, ASID, June Roesslein Interiors, Chesterfield, MO (bottom)

p. 89: © Alise O'Brien Photography; design: Barbara Slavkin, Allied Member, ASID, June Roesslein Interiors, Chesterfield, MO

p. 91: © 2003 Sylvia Martin Photographer; design: Mike McKay, CGR, CAPS, Oak Alley, Inc., Birmingham, AL

p. 92: © 2004 Brian Vanden Brink, Photographer (top left and bottom); © David Duncan Livingston (right)

p. 93: © Scot Zimmerman Photography; design: Chris Evans, 2 Design, St. George, UT (top left and right); © Mark Samu/Samu Studios Inc.; design: Durst Construction, Charlton, NY (bottom left and right)

p. 94: © Randy O'Rourke (left top and bottom); © Robert Perron; design: Svigals + Partners Architects, New Haven, CT (right top); © 2003 Brian Vanden Brink, Photographer; design: Reed & Co. Architecture, Portland, ME (right bottom)

p. 95: Courtesy Orfield Design & Construction; design: Orfield Design & Construction, Inc., Edina, MN

p. 96: © Kerry Hayes; design: D'Arcy Dunal Architect, Toronto, Ontario, Canada (left); © Mark Samu/Samu Studios Inc.; design: Kate Johns, AIA, Old Chatham, NY (center); © Dana Davis; design: On the Beam

Remodeling, Inc., Oakland, CA (right)

p. 97: © 2004 Brian Vanden Brink, Photographer; design: Christopher Campbell Architecture, Portland, ME (left); © Joe Witt; design: Charley Ingle, Sopchoppy, FL (center); © Ken Gutmaker; design: Susan Thabit, Balboa Island, CA, and Doug Root, Premiere Woodworks, Newport Beach, CA (right)

p. 98–99: © Chipper Hatter; design: Archway Construction Services, Inc., Alpharetta, GA; Mamdani Design, LLC, Atlanta, GA

p. 100: Courtesy Urbieta Construction, Inc.

p. 101: © Tom Lehman; design: Urbieta Construction, Inc., Dayton, OH

p. 103: Courtesy Benjamin Nutter Associates Architects; design: Ben Nutter, AIA, Benjamin Nutter Associates Architects, Topsfield, MA (top and bottom left); courtesy of MTI Whirlpools (bottom right)

p. 104: Courtesy Norene Sakazaki, Harrell Remodeling (top); © Ken Gutmaker; design: Ryan J. Seyfert, Harrell Remodeling, Inc., Mountain View, CA, Madalyn Baker, Design & Interiors, Los Altos, CA (bottom)

p. 105: © Ken Gutmaker; design: Ryan J. Seyfert, Harrell Remodeling, Inc., Mountain View, CA, Madalyn Baker, Design & Interiors, Los Altos, CA

p. 106-107: © Mark Samu/Samu Studios Inc.; design: Kate Johns, AIA, Old Chatham, NY

p. 109: © Kerry Hayes; design: D'Arcy Dunal Architect, Toronto, Ontario, Canada

p. 110: © Philip Clayton-Thompson Photography; design: Styling by Donna Pizzi (left); © 2004 Brian Vanden Brink, Photographer; design: Christopher Campbell Architecture, Portland, ME (top right); © David Duncan Livingston (bottom right)

p. 111: © Dana Davis; design: On the Beam Remodeling, Inc., Oakland, CA (left); Ken Vaughn Photography; design: D&D Remodel/ Design, Irving, TX (right)

p. 112: © Timothy Bell Photography; design: Jim Rill and Jon Reinhard, Rill & Decker Architects, Bethesda, MD (left); © Roger Turk, Northlight Photography; design: Christopher Saxman, Christopher Saxman Architect, Oak Harbor, WA; construction: Yonkman Construction Inc., Oak Harbor, WA (right)

p. 113: © Ken Gutmaker; design: Susan Thabit, Balboa Island, CA, and Doug Root, Premiere Woodworks, Newport Beach, CA (left); Joe Witt; design: Charley Ingle, Sopchoppy, FL (right)

p. 114: James Maidhof Photography; design: Rhino Builders, Inc., Kansas City, KS (left); courtesy Orfield Design & Construction; design: Orfield Design & Construction, Inc., Edina, MN (center); courtesy Case Design/ Remodeling, Alain Jaramillo Photography; design: Rick and Susan Matus, Case Design/ Remodeling, Inc., Bethesda, MD (right)

p. 115: Courtesy Michael Pettersen Associates (left); © Tria Giovan Photography (center); © Grey Crawford; design: Tom Douglas, Seattle, WA (right)

p. 116: © Chipper Hatter (top); James Maidhof Photography; design: Rhino Builders, Inc., Kansas City, KS (bottom)

p. 117: James Maidhof Photography; design: Rhino Builders, Inc., Kansas City, KS

p. 118: Courtesy Orfield Design & Construction

p. 119: Courtesy Orfield Design & Construction; design: Orfield Design & Construction, Inc., Edina, MN

p. 120: Courtesy Case Design/Remodeling, Alain Jaramillo Photography; design: Rick and Susan Matus, Case Design/Remodeling, Inc., Bethesda, MD

p. 121: Courtesy Case Design/Remodeling, Alain Jaramillo Photography; design: Rick and Susan Matus, Case Design/Remodeling, Inc., Bethesda, MD (left); © Warren Bond; design: Andy Spaugh, Hammerhead Home Improvement, Atlanta, GA (right)

p. 123: Courtesy Michael Pettersen Associates (left); © Mark Samu/Samu Studios Inc., design: Lucianna Samu (right)

p. 124: © Tria Giovan Photography (top left); © Robert Perron; design: Interdesign Limited, Old Lyme, CT (top right); © Carolyn L. Bates; design: Sandra Vitzthum Architect, LLC, Montpelier, VT (bottom)

p. 125: © Mark Samu/Samu Studios Inc., design: Kathrine F. McCoy, AIA., Architect, Bridgehampton, NY (top left); © Grey Crawford; design: Tom Douglas, Seattle, WA (top right); © Roger Turk/Northlight Photography, Inc., design: Crafted Interiors, Seattle, WA (bottom)

p. 126: © 2002 Brian Vanden Brink, Photographer; design: Stephen Blatt Architects, Portland, ME

p. 127: © 2003 Brian Vanden Brink, Photographer; design: John Cole Architect, Arlington, MA, and Fryeburg, ME (top); © Grey Crawford; design: Josh Heitler, Lacina Group, New York, NY (bottom left); © Jessie Walker (bottom right)

p. 128: Courtesy Michael Hewes & Co.; design: Michael Hewes and Ric Pomillia, Michael Hewes & Co., Blue Hill, ME, and Peter d'Entremont, Knight Associates, Architects, Blue Hill, ME (left); © Randy O'Rourke; design: Mark T. White, CKD, Kitchen Encounters, Annapolis, MD; custom carpenter: Dallas Jones (center); © Seth Tice-Lewis; design: Giles Blunden, Blunden Piesse Architects, Carrboro, NC; construction: Chandler Design-Build, Chapel Hill, NC (right)

p. 129: © Jason Selznick; design: Don Nathan, Floyd, VA (left); © Phillip Ennis Photography; design: Andrew R. Chary, Chary & Sigenza Architects, LLP, Lake Placid and Bedford, NY (center); © Joe Gayle Photography; design: Brothers Strong, Inc., Houston, TX (right)

p. 130: Courtesy Knight Associates, Architects (top); © Robert Perron; design: Michael Hewes and Ric Pomillia, Michael Hewes & Co., Blue Hill, ME, and Peter d'Entremont, Knight Associates, Architects, Blue Hill, ME (bottom)

p. 131: © Robert Perron; design: Michael Hewes and Ric Pomillia, Michael Hewes & Co., Blue Hill, ME, and Peter d'Entremont, Knight Associates, Architects, Blue Hill, ME

p. 132: © Randy O'Rourke; design: Mark T. White, CKD, Kitchen Encounters, Annapolis, MD; custom carpenter: Dallas Jones

p. 133: © Randy O'Rourke; design: Mark T. White, CKD, Kitchen Encounters, Annapolis, MD; custom carpenter: Dallas Jones (left); © Anthony Tripp; design: Don Van Cura Construction Co., Chicago, IL (right)

p. 134: © Seth Tice-Lewis; design: Giles Blunden, Blunden Piesse Architects, Carrboro, NC; construction: Chandler Design-Build, Chapel Hill, NC

p. 135: © Seth Tice-Lewis; design: Giles Blunden, Blunden Piesse Architects, Carrboro, NC; construction: Chandler Design-Build, Chapel Hill, NC (left); design: Black + Vernooy Architecture and Urban Design, Austin, TX (right)

p. 137: © Jason Selznick; design: Don Nathan, Floyd, VA

p. 139: © Phillip Ennis Photography; design: Andrew R. Chary, Chary & Sigenza Architects, LLP, Lake Placid and Bedford, NY

p. 140: © Ken Gutmaker; design: Susan Thabit; construction: John Washer, Cabinets Plus, Irvine, CA

p. 141: © Mary Ludington; design: Sarah Susanka, FAIA, while with Mulfinger, Susanka, Mahady & Partners (top); © Joe Gayle Photography; design: Brothers Strong, Inc., Houston, TX (bottom left and right)

p. 142: © Grey Crawford; design: Rick and Deann Bayless, Chicago, IL (left top and bottom); John Hermannsson; design: John Hermannsson, Hermannsson Architects, Redwood City, CA (right)

p. 143: Charles Wilkins; design: Kay Green Design, Inc., Orlando, FL, Ryland Homes, Tampa Division (left); © 2003 Brian Vanden Brink, Photographer; design: Dominic Paul Mercadante Architecture, Belfast, ME (right)

p. 144: © Paul Gates; design: Rob Whitehead, AIA, and Kelly Roberson, Des Moines, IA (left); © Chipper Hatter; design: Stephanie Ives; intern architect/residential designer, Marietta, GA; construction: Russell Ives, Marietta, GA (center); © Andrew MacIver; design: Donna Schratwieser, Djs Interiors, Mt. Laurel, NJ (right)

p. 145: © Jessie Walker; design: Richard Becker, AIA, Becker Architects Ltd., Highland Park, IL; cabinetry: Exclusive Woodworking, Waukegan, IL (left); © 2004 Brian Vanden

Brink, Photographer; design: Robert Knight and Dominic Mercadante, Knight Associates, Architects, Blue Hill, ME; carpentry: Ruger Associates, Blue Hill, ME (center); © Eric Roth; design: Thomas Buckborough, Thomas Buckborough and Associates, Concord, MA (right)

p. 146: Courtesy Rob Whitehead

p. 147–149: © Paul Gates; design: Rob Whitehead, AIA, and Kelly Roberson, Des Moines, IA

p. 150: Courtesy Stephanie Ives

p. 151–153: © Chipper Hatter; design: Stephanie Ives, intern architect/residential designer, Marietta, GA; construction: Russell Ives, Marietta, GA

p. 154: © Andrew MacIver; design: Donna Schratwieser, Djs Interiors, Mt. Laurel, NJ

p. 155: © Andrew MacIver; design: Donna Schratwieser, Djs Interiors, Mt. Laurel, NJ (top); William Wood, McKinney Architects; design: Al Wood, AIA, McKinney Architects, Inc., Austin, TX (bottom)

p. 156–157: © Andrew MacIver; design: Donna Schratwieser, Djs Interiors, Mt. Laurel, NJ

p. 159: © Jessie Walker; design: Richard Becker, AIA, Becker Architects Ltd., Highland Park, IL; cabinetry: Exclusive Woodworking, Waukegan, IL

p. 161: © 2004 Brian Vanden Brink, Photographer; design: Robert Knight and Dominic Mercadante, Knight Associates, Architects, Blue Hill, ME; carpentry: Ruger Associates, Blue Hill, ME

p. 162: Courtesy Thomas Buckborough and Associates

p. 163: © Eric Roth; design: Thomas Buckborough, Thomas Buckborough and Associates, Concord, MA

p. 164: © Philip Beaurline; design: Architects Allison Ewing and Chris Hayes, Christopher Hayes Design Studio, Charlottesville, VA (left); © David Duncan Livingston; design: House + House Architects and Touché Design, San Francisco, CA (top right); © 2002 Brian Vanden Brink, Photographer; design: Joe Waltman, Anastos & Nadeau, Builders and Designers, Yarmouth, ME (bottom right)

p. 165: © 2004 Norman McGrath, design: Amy Finlay Scott, New York, NY

p. 166: © 2003 Brian Vanden Brink, Photographer; design: Polemus Savery DaSilva Architects Builders, Chatham and Osterville, MA (top left); © Timothy Bell Photography; design: Jim Rill, Rill & Decker Architects, Bethesda, MD (top right); © Paul Bardagjy/Through the Lens Mgt., Inc.; design: Webber Hanzlik Architects, Austin, TX (bottom left); © Susan Gilmore; design: Orfield Design & Construction, Inc., Edina, MN (bottom right)

p. 167: © 2003 Sargent; design: Marc-Michaels Interior Design, Inc., Winter Park, FL